Treasures
of
the Father's
LOVE

365 Daily Devotions

GINA LYNN MURRAY

Treasures of the Father's Love
365 Daily Devotions
©2022 Gina Lynn Murray
All rights reserved.

Publishing Assistant: Ellen Sallas, www.theauthorsmentor.com
Front Cover © DepositPhotos.com/Wacomka
Softcover ISBN 979-8-9858673-3-6 | V10232022SC
Also available in hardcover and eBook publication

info@findingrestmin.org | www.findingrestmin.org

PUBLISHED IN THE UNITED STATES OF AMERICA

Dedication

I dedicate this book to my Father, my Abba, my Daddy God. Without His love I would not be where I am today, or who I am today. His extravagant love for me is the very air I breathe.   Also, to my earthly dad who has sacrificed many times to show his family true love.

The Lord your God is in your midst,
a Mighty One who will save;
He will rejoice over you with gladness;
He will quiet you by His love;
He will exult over you
with loud singing.

Zephaniah 3:17 ESV

Treasures of the Father's Love

My purpose in writing this daily devotional is to pour the love of God into broken vessels. I want to shout from the rooftops of the Father's love for you. I have come to know Him as Father. I want His children to know He is not mad at them. He is extravagantly in love with you.

He has written over and over in His Word how much He loves you. He wants to pour His love on you. He wants to take care of you. I pray that as you read through each devotion, you will begin to know and believe the love the Father has for you and that His love will start to heal broken hearts and mend wounds. I hope that at the end of the 365 days, you will know your Father in a way you never dreamed possible.

I pray you will know His character, that He is kind and gentle. He is compassionate and tender. He is not hard or harsh or waiting to punish you, but He wants to bless you and have intimacy with you with all His heart. You are His beloved.

DAY 1

Stay Focused

We do this by keeping our eyes on Jesus, the champion who initiates and perfects our faith. Because of the joy awaiting him, he endured the cross, disregarding its shame. Now he is seated in the place of honor beside God's throne.
Hebrews 12:2 NLT

God calls you to keep your eyes on Jesus, the Author, and the Perfector of your faith. He endured the cross because of the joy awaiting Him. You were that joy. He endured the taunts and the beatings; He took the nails in His hands and feet because He knew that waiting on the other side of the pain of the cross was a relationship with you. He didn't worry about how it looked to others or if they were pleased with Him. He didn't worry about if it was going to bring shame to Him. He loved you so much that He took it all with joy. Remember today in whatever you face, that you can face it with joy when you keep your eyes fixed on Jesus who loves you more than you can imagine. The One who is now seated at the right hand of the Father. The One who awaits in anticipation to pour His love out on you.

DAY 2

He Sings Over You

*For the Lord your God is living among you. He is a
mighty Savior. He will take delight in you with gladness.
With His love He will calm all your fears. He will rejoice
over you with joyful songs.*
Zephaniah 3:17 NLT

God loves you so much, and you are His great delight. He
is always with you, right beside you, watching over you
and protecting your every move. He calms all your fears
with His perfect, unconditional, unimaginable love. When
you know how much He loves you, you know you can trust
Him with every single detail of your life. He always has
the best of intentions for you. He rejoices every time He
sees your face. He sings a new song over your life every
single morning. He is your kind and compassionate Father
who will never, ever, for one moment abandon you or
reject you. He is yours, and you are His forever. Live each
day out of His love for you. He does not love you according
to your behavior, but He loves you regardless of your
behavior because He wants to love you. He created you to
love. He will always love you. He is pleased with you and
proud of you. Hold your head high because you are His
child, and you are highly honored and dearly loved!

DAY 3

Drink Deep From The Fountain Of Life

You give them drink from your river of delights. For with you is the fountain of life; in your light we see light.
Psalm 36:8-9 NIV

When you drink deep Jesus, and His living water, you will never thirst again. It satisfies every single part of your being. He is the Fountain of Life, and He gives you abundant life. A life that is free and whole, that you could never even dream of. He is the light that guides each step of your way. He will never leave you or forsake you. He invites you to drink deeply of Him every day and experience this abundant life. Take a deep drink today. Savor the moments in His presence. Let that Living Water from the Fountain of Life wash over every part of you. Let it heal your mind and your soul. Let it mend your broken heart and be like healing oil throughout your entire being. Drink freely and deeply from the Fountain of Jesus. You will never thirst again.

DAY 4

Made In God's Image

So God created human beings in his own image. In the image of God, he created them; male and female, he created them. Then God looked over all he had made, and he saw that it was very good!
Genesis 1:26; 31 NLT

When God looks at you, He sees a masterpiece. He sees an exquisite sight. Of all the things He created, you are His absolute favorite! You were created in His very image. He wanted you to exist.

Never doubt your worth or your existence. You are not an accident. God planned for you before the foundations of the earth. He then looked at you and didn't just say it is good; He said it is VERY good! He is enthralled with you. He adores you, and He brags to all creation about you. Square your shoulders, raise your head high, and walk with confidence because you are made in God's image! You are loved!

DAY 5

Jesus Leads You Out

My beloved speaks and says to me:
"Arise, my love, my beautiful one,
and come away,
Song of Songs 2:10 ESV

When you call to God, He hears your voice. Even the tiniest whisper gets His attention. He leans forward to press in to listen to you. He calls you to come away with Him. He wants you to rest in Him. Spend time with Him. He loves these moments with you. He draws you close to His chest and whispers His love into your ear. He calls you, His beloved. His treasure. He loves to pour out His blessings on you. Now is the time! There is no need to wait until you think you have it all together or until you feel like you can come before Him without shame. Now, every moment of every day is the time. He is always attentive to your cries; your voice sounds beautiful to His ears. He calls you His beautiful one. His prized possession. Take the time to lean into His chest and let Him love you today. You will walk away from those moments refreshed like never before. You are His beloved!

5

DAY 6

God Thinks About You

*How precious are your thoughts about me, O God.
They cannot be numbered! I can't even count them;
they outnumber the grains of sand!
And when I wake up, you are still with me!*
Psalm 139:17-18 NLT

God is thinking about you every single moment of every single day. You are the focus of His mind, and He cherishes you. He has nothing but good and kind desires toward you. If you could count the grains of sand on every shore, which is impossible, His thoughts for you even outnumber those. He is consistently thinking of ways to pour His love on you, to care for you, to show Himself faithful to you. God wants you to know Him in a real and tangible way. Before you open your eyes in the morning, He is already there thinking about you. Before you close your eyes at night, and while you are sleeping His thoughts are towards you. Today do not allow feelings of insignificance to overwhelm you because you are on His mind. He is the Creator of the Universe, and He is madly in love with you.

DAY 7

God Is Coming

With this news, strengthen those who have tired hands, and encourage those who have weak knees. Say to those with fearful hearts, "Be strong, and do not fear, for your God is coming to destroy your enemies. He is coming to save you."
Isaiah 35:3-4 NLT

Be strong and do not fear. Fear can be paralyzing. It can make you think you will never make it. Fear wants to blind you to God's love and care for you. It is easy to say do not fear, but it is harder to follow through. Understanding who God is and how much He loves you gives you the courage to face whatever may come your way. When your hands feel tired and your knees feel weak, look up to God. He is coming to save you and to destroy the enemy of fear in your life. Let His love cause you to look fear in the eye and move forward in whatever it is He ask you to do today.

7

DAY 8

Rest In Jesus' Unforced Rhythms Of Grace

*"Are you tired? Worn out? Burned out on religion?
Come to me. Get away with me, and you'll recover your
life. I'll show you how to take a real rest. Walk with me
and work with me—watch how I do it. Learn the unforced
rhythms of grace. I won't lay anything heavy or ill-fitting
on you. Keep company with me and you'll learn to live
freely and lightly."*
Matthew 11:28-30 MSG

Jesus invites you to get away with Him and rest. To recover
your life. It is only in Him that you learn to take a real rest.
As you walk with Him and watch how He does life, you
will learn to walk freely and lightly with unforced rhythms
in your life. He will show you the right rhythms for
you. What is suitable for others may not be right for you.
He knows you and loves you, and He knows exactly what
you need to be able to rest. Today if you are tired and
burned out, take His invitation, and walk with Him to a
place of rest. Rest in His love for you. Rest in His grace
and mercy in your life. Let the striving and frustration of
trying to fix everything cease.

DAY 9

Be Refreshed

"Come, everyone who thirsts, come to the waters;
and he who has no money, come, buy and eat!
Come, buy wine and milk without money and without
price. Why do you spend your money for that which is not
bread, and your labor for that which does not satisfy?
Listen diligently to me, and eat what is good,
and delight yourselves in rich food.
Isaiah 55:1-2 ESV

Jesus satisfies your hunger and your thirst with His refreshing water. You don't have to be rich or important to drink this water. Greater than the finest of foods and the finest of drink, Jesus pours out Himself for you. Greater than any material thing is a relationship with Him. He does not turn away anyone. He accepts any race, color, and economic status. He wants to refresh you and love you. He feeds more than your body; He feeds your soul, the very core of who you are. He invites you to drink deeply of this water and enjoy the feast of who He is. Start your day with a long drink of the finest water you will ever find. Take a bite of the richest food you could ever taste. Taste and see that He is good. Take a long, long drink and savor Him.

DAY 10

You Are Abundantly Free

Because of the sacrifice of the Messiah, his blood poured out on the altar of the Cross, we're a free people—free of penalties and punishments chalked up by all our misdeeds. And not just barely free, either, abundantly free! He thought of everything, provided for everything we could possibly need, letting us in on the plans he took such delight in making. He set it all out before us in Christ, a long-range plan in which everything would be brought together and summed up in him, everything in deepest heaven, everything on planet earth.
Ephesians 1:7-10 MSG

Jesus poured out His blood on the cross because of the Father's great love for you. With that blood, He purchased your freedom and set you, not just a little free, but abundantly free! You are no longer punished for your sins when you become God's child because Jesus took the punishment for you on the cross. He provided at that moment for absolutely everything you would ever need. He took delight in making plans for you. He is delighted in you, He smiles over you, and you are so loved. As you go about your day today, remember that you have everything you need in Jesus to live the life God has put before you to live. As you live that life, remember it gave God delight to plan it for you.

10

DAY 11

God Calls You & Preserves You

Listen to me, O coastlands, and give attention, you peoples from afar. The Lord called me from the womb, from the body of my mother he named my name. He made my mouth like a sharp sword; in the shadow of his hand he hid me; he made me a polished arrow; in his quiver he hid me away.
Isaiah 49:1-2 ESV

God has a purpose for you. A plan that is greater than you could ever imagine. Before you were even born, He knew that purpose. Before your mother knew your name, He had already named you. He called you beloved, chosen, royal priest, a precious masterpiece. You are His prized possession. God has you hidden away and protected under His mighty hand until He knows the timing is perfect for releasing you into what He has called you to. During that time, God is preparing you for what He already has prepared for you. He has gone ahead of you and made the way. He already knows what doors need to be opened and when to open them. Rest in who He says you are and in His perfect timing. Nothing is wasted in your life. God will use it all. Stay where He has you until the time is right, and He will bring you out of hiding.

DAY 12

God Goes Before You

*"It is the Lord who goes before you. He will be with you;
he will not leave you or forsake you. Do not fear or be
dismayed."*
Deuteronomy 31:8 ESV

God always goes before you in everything you do. He
always prepares the way for you. He plans for everything
and prepares for everything according to His great love for
you. He always has the best of intentions for you. He will
never abandon you along the way; He will walk with you.
He is right beside you, holding you by His hand. You do
not ever have to be afraid or discouraged. Whatever it is
today that you are facing, know that He has gone before
you. He has already opened the doors that need to be
opened and closed those He does not want you to walk
through. He sends you signs and warnings along the way,
and He points you down the right paths. Whether it is a job
interview, a doctor's appointment, or a trip to the grocery
store, He has already been there. Rest in Him.

DAY 13

God Is Your Shelter

*Those who live in the shelter of the Most High, will find
rest in the shadow of the Almighty.
This I declare about the Lord: He alone is my refuge, my
place of safety; he is my God, and I trust him.*
Psalm 91:1-2 NLT

God is your shelter. Run to Him and find rest under the
shadow of His wings. He will be your place of safety and
protection whenever you need Him. He is trustworthy and
true. He will be faithful to fulfill His promises to you. You
can count on Him. He will hide you in His secret place
when everything is raging around you. You can call on
Him, and He will answer you. He will be with you. He will
never abandon you in your time of need. God alone is your
God. He alone will be your refuge in the time of trouble.
He loves you, and He will watch over you. He will hide
you and protect you. Run to God today when you feel
overwhelmed and like everything is falling apart. He loves
you. He will wrap His love around you like a warm
blanket.

DAY 14

God Knew You

"I knew you before I formed you in your mother's womb.
Before you were born I set you apart
and appointed you as my prophet to the nations."
Jeremiah 1:5 NLT

Before your parents ever thought of you, long before you were even formed in the womb, God knew you. God knew everything about you before you were ever born. He knew every decision you would make, the color of your hair and your personality. He knew you intimately. He knew your likes and your dislikes. He knew every single detail about you down to the tiniest one, and yet God loved you. He loves every part of you. Before you were ever born, He set you apart. He had a plan for your life before you were even conceived. A plan you could never comprehend or imagine in your wildest dreams. God has chosen you. You are His.

DAY 15

Approach God With Confidence

*Therefore, since we have a great high priest who has
ascended into heaven, Jesus the Son of God, let us hold
firmly to the faith we profess. For we do not have a high
priest who is unable to empathize with our weaknesses,
but we have one who has been tempted in every way, just
as we are—yet he did not sin. Let us then approach God's
throne of grace with confidence, so that we may receive
mercy and find grace to help us in our time of need.*
Hebrews 4:14-16 NIV

Hold firmly to what you believe about God. Do not let anyone
talk you out of it. Do not be discouraged when you face
troubles or temptations because Jesus faced them too. He
knows your weaknesses and understands the fight that you
fight, He fought with the same temptations to go beyond the
boundaries. Temptations to quit. Temptations to let what
people think matter more than what God thinks. And yet, He
did not give in to these. Because He did not give in and He
faced the cross, you can come with boldness and confidence
straight into the Holy Place. You can approach Him and
receive His mercy and grace freely. Ask Him for help when
you need it. The veil was torn, and nothing separates you
from Him. God loves having this time with you. Place all
your trust in Him and approach Him, believing He loves you
and wants to help you. Come boldly and with confidence
today and bring all your needs to Him.

DAY 16

God Will Fight For You

But Moses told the people, "Don't be afraid. Just stand where you are and watch, and you will see the wonderful way the Lord will rescue you today. The Egyptians you are looking at—you will never see them again. The Lord will fight for you, and you won't need to lift a finger!"
Exodus 14:13-14 TLB

Do not spend all your time striving and trying to figure everything out. The enemy wants to distract you and throw up smokescreens, getting you to fight battles that have no meaning. Jesus has already defeated the powers of darkness. He has rescued you and made you whole. Don't let the enemy distract you from the most important thing by chasing rabbit trails. Look at the finished work of Jesus, it is your victory! When the enemy comes roaring like a lion in your ears, resist Him, by trusting in God, focusing on God, and resting in God. The enemy has no power to harm you. Don't let the fear overwhelm you. Fear likes to be loud and make you think he can harm you, but fear is a liar. God is Greater, and He is with you and in you. You have absolutely nothing to fear.

DAY 17

God Sees You Even In The Dark

*I could ask the darkness to hide me and the light around
me to become night—but even in darkness I cannot hide
from you. To you the night shines as bright as day.
Darkness and light are the same to you.*
Psalm 139:11-12 NLT

There is not one place you can hide that God is not there
with you, watching over you. Even when darkness
surrounds you, it is still light to God. He is Light and Life.
There are times that you feel shame and run from Him, but
He will still pursue you. God's love will never stop chasing
you. He will never abandon you or fail you. Run to Him,
do not run away from Him. When you feel unworthy, God
still wants to comfort you. He still wants you to run to
Him. Let His light shine in your darkness. Know that you
could never do anything that would turn His face from
you. He stands with open arms no matter what you have
done or where you have been.

DAY 18

God Will Rescue You From Darkness

God rescued us from dead-end alleys and dark dungeons.
He's set us up in the kingdom of the Son he loves so
much, the Son who got us out of the pit we were in, got
rid of the sins we were doomed to keep repeating.
Colossians 1:13-14 MSG

Jesus steps into the darkest dungeons and the deepest pits
with you, and He pulls you out. He pulls you out of the
darkness and sets you into His glorious light through His
sacrifice. He rescues you from your sins and puts your feet
on solid ground. There is no dungeon too dark, no pit too
deep, no place too far, that Jesus cannot find you and
rescue you. Sometimes you are in a pit because of
something you have done yourself. Sometimes because of
something someone else has done, but no matter what got
you there, He will never leave you there. He will never give
up on you. You will never wear out His love or His
patience for you.

DAY 19

God Is Your Help.

I look up to the mountains—does my help come from there? My help comes from the Lord, who made heaven and earth! He will not let you stumble; the one who watches over you will not slumber. Indeed, he who watches over Israel never slumbers or sleeps.
Psalm 121:1-4 NLT

When life seems to be shaking around you, and the darkness is closing in on you, look up! God is your help. No man can take care of you the way that He can. He created everything in heaven and on earth, and He will take care of you. Nothing is impossible for God. He has access to everything He needs to help you. He can create something out of nothing if He needs to. He can change molecular structures if He needs to. Trust your life in His hands. He will keep a firm grip on you. He never closes His eyes to sleep because His eyes are always watching out for you.

DAY 20

He Will Show You Where To Go

Trust in the Lord with all your heart; do not depend on your own understanding. Seek his will in all you do, and he will show you which path to take.
Proverbs 3:5-6 NLT

Trust in God. He knows exactly what He is doing. You do not need to figure it all out. Don't think that you know it all. Let go of having to be in control of everything. God loves you. He knows what is best for you. He will make perfect decisions for your life. Every single decision God makes for you is made from His heart of love for you. Seek His face. Seek His will, and He will show you which paths you should take. He will show you which doors you should walk through. He will bring the right people into your life to walk alongside you in specific seasons. Do not let yourself fret and worry when you cannot see a way out because God already knows the way out. He has already gone before you and prepared the way for you. Trust in Him because He loves you.

DAY 21

You Have Right Standing

Who dares accuse us whom God has chosen for his own?
Will God? No! He is the one who has forgiven us and
given us right standing with himself. Who then will
condemn us? Will Christ? No! For he is the one who died
for us and came back to life again for us and is sitting at
the place of highest honor next to God, pleading for us
there in heaven.
Romans 8:33-34 TLB

God has chosen you; why would He then accuse you? He sent Jesus to be the sacrifice for your sins to give you right standing with Him. When you are in Christ, there is no longer any condemnation. When man tries to accuse you, God sees your heart. He knows the truth about you. He loves you, and He forgives you once and for all. He throws your sins into the sea of forgetfulness to be remembered no more. Jesus sits at the right hand of the Father. He is seated in a place of highest honor, and He is continually interceding for you. Jesus is your advocate. God is always waiting with open arms for you to turn to Him. The moment you ask for forgiveness, you receive it immediately. God doesn't wait for you to get it all together; the moment you call His name, He runs to your rescue. He is always here for you, always attentive to your prayers. You are so very loved.

DAY 22

God Is At Your Right Hand

*I have set the Lord always before me; because he is at my
right hand, I shall not be shaken.
Therefore my heart is glad, and my whole being rejoices;
my flesh also dwells secure.*
Psalm 16:8-9 ESV

Seek God's face. Set it before you every day, in every
situation in your life. He will always be at your side. You
will never walk this journey alone. When you look behind
you, and before you, you will see Him. You will be able to
see His handprint in the details of your life. If you always
put His face before you, you will not be shaken. He is
unshakeable. He is a firm and steady foundation. He puts
joy in your heart, and His joy becomes your strength daily.
If you will trust God and do not try to figure everything out
on your own, you will dwell securely in this world. In this
world, you will have troubles, but make God's love your
firm foundation, and you will always walk in peace no
matter what the circumstances that are swirling around
you. He is your Safe Place. He is your Tower of Refuge
and Strength. You can always run to God, and He will
always receive you with open arms. Whatever you face this
day, invite God in. He loves to live life with you.

DAY 23

Jesus Won It All

But He was wounded for our transgressions, He was bruised for our guilt and iniquities; the chastisement [needful to obtain] peace and well-being for us was upon Him, and with the stripes [that wounded] Him we are healed and made whole.
Isaiah 53:5 AMPC

Jesus went to a cross on your behalf. There is nothing you must do to appease God or earn His affections. Jesus has already done everything that needs to be done. He took your guilt and shame and nailed it to the cross. He endured everything because of His great love for you. He was bruised to take away your guilt and sins. He was chastised so that you could have peace and say it is well with your soul. He took the stripes on His back so that you could be healed and made whole, not just physically, but spiritually, mentally, and emotionally. You are complete in Jesus. He didn't have to die, but He chose to die. He chose to be separated from God on the cross because He wanted a relationship with you. As you go through your day, remember that it is finished. Jesus has done absolutely everything that needs to be done. He did it not so God would love you, but because God already loved you. You are complete.

DAY 24

God Will Never Withhold His Love

*Lord, don't hold back your tender mercies from me. Let
your unfailing love and faithfulness always protect me.*
Psalm 40:11 NLT

God will never withhold anything from you that is in your
best interest. He always has the best of intentions at heart for
you. God daily pours out His love and tender mercies on you.
If you are praying for something and do not see the answers,
don't ever give up. God sees things ahead that you cannot see,
and He knows things about your future that you do not know.
Trust God in the silence. He is always faithful to you. He can
never be anything but faithful. There may be prayers He is
not answering because of some reason that He can see, and
you can't; He is protecting you from something that is not
best for you. Don't think that God doesn't love you just
because you haven't seen the answer yet. He may not be
saying no; He may just be saying wait for the perfect timing.
God's promises are always fulfilled. It may not be in the way
you thought it would be or look like you thought it would
look, but if He made you a promise, He will fulfill it. He
cannot and will not ever lie to you. You can trust God
completely. Remember that nothing is too hard for Him.
Keep a lookout for ways that He may be answering your
prayers that you are not seeing. It isn't always in the big or
obvious ways; sometimes, it is in the simple ways. Each day
He sends little pieces of His love your way. Look up today!

DAY 25

God Can Do Anything

*God can do anything, you know—far more than you could
ever imagine or guess or request in your wildest dreams!
He does it not by pushing us around but by working
within us, his Spirit deeply and gently within us. Glory to
God in the church! Glory to God in the Messiah, in
Jesus! Glory down all the generations! Glory through all
millennia! Oh, yes!*
Ephesians 3:20-21 MSG

God can do absolutely anything! Nothing is ever too hard
for Him; He is the God of the impossible. He can do way
above and beyond anything, you could ever imagine, ask
for, or dream about, even in your wildest dreams. He
cannot be put in a box, and there are no limits on Him. God
controls even the cosmos. He is the Creator of everything
in heaven and on earth. All He must do is speak one word,
and things are made that did not even exist. He rearranges
molecules and atoms. He creates new cells.

He is God, and there is no other. There is nothing that you
ask for or need in your life that He cannot do. His very
Spirit, the same Spirit that raised Jesus from the dead, lives
inside of you when you are His child. His Spirit works
deeply within you.

25

God never pushes you around, but He is gentle and kind as He transforms you. Why would you ever worry about anything when you realize who your Father is and that He flung the stars in the skies and told the oceans how far they could go. He is with you! He is always for you! Dare to dream big dreams, knowing that He can do even bigger! He loves to leave you awestruck.

DAY 26

Why Would You Doubt?

But when he saw the strong wind and the waves, he was terrified and began to sink. "Save me, Lord!" he shouted. Jesus immediately reached out and grabbed him. "You have so little faith," Jesus said.
"Why did you doubt me?"
Matthew 14:30-31 NLT

The moment you cry out to God, He moves toward you. His ears are always attentive to your voice. No matter the situation or circumstances causing you to call on Him, He will never be angry with you. Even if you have gotten into a situation that you cannot get yourself out of, He will still help you. He will not judge you or condemn you in any way. He is kind and compassionate. God will always reach out and grab you. He will pull you up out of any pit. Do not let the winds and waves around you cause you to question His love and faithfulness to you. The doubt will whisper to you that God doesn't care and that He won't come through for you. It will tell you that you cannot let go and trust Him, but doubt is a liar. God is always trustworthy!

DAY 27

God Is There In Your Need

"The poor and homeless are desperate for water, their tongues parched and no water to be found. But I'm there to be found, I'm there for them, and I, God of Israel, will not leave them thirsty. I'll open up rivers for them on the barren hills, spout fountains in the valleys. I'll turn the baked-clay badlands into a cool pond, the waterless waste into splashing creeks. I'll plant the red cedar in that treeless wasteland, also acacia, myrtle, and olive. I'll place the cypress in the desert, with plenty of oaks and pines. Everyone will see this. No one can miss it— unavoidable, indisputable evidence, That I, God, personally did this. It's created and signed by The Holy of Israel.
Isaiah 41:17-20 MSG

God's heart is always toward the hurting. He will never leave them in their time of need. God's love always moves Him to help. He has many resources to help. His hope is that because you have received His love, you will also let the needs of the hurting move your heart. You can do many things to try to please Him, but what pleases Him most is when you reach out to the poor and the needy. Bring water to the thirsty and the lonely. Feed the orphans and widows. When you do these things, you show people who He is. You show them God's heart for them. God will always take care of you. He can open rivers and make ponds in the desert.

Nothing is impossible for God, and as you show His love to others, He will do these miracles through you. They will know that He is the One doing these things. No man can do the things God will do when you are working with Him to fulfill His purposes on earth.

DAY 28

God Is Faithful

Trust in the LORD, and do good;
dwell in the land and befriend faithfulness.
Psalm 37:3 ESV

You can trust God with every detail of your life. As you
trust in Him, seek His righteousness, and He will take care
of your needs. Keep your eyes on God. Amidst your daily
life, when things seem hard, bring to your remembrance
God's promises to you. Fix your heart on them, knowing
that He will never fail you. God is trustworthy and faithful.
He will do what He has promised. Even if you don't see
the promise yet, wait for it, believe for it, expect it. God's
faithful promises are the solid ground for you to stand on.
Do not let doubt steal His promises away from you. He is
your Father, and His heart for you is always for your
best. Feast on His faithfulness each day.

DAY 29

The Truth Will Set You Free

So Jesus said to the Jews who had believed him, "If you abide in my word, you are truly my disciples, and you will know the truth, and the truth will set you free."
John 8:31-32 ESV

When you abide in God's Word, you abide in Him. Jesus is the Word made flesh. He is the Way, the Truth, and the Life. When you abide in Jesus, you get to know His character. You begin to understand His love for you. You begin to hear Him whisper your identity to you. As you start to realize who God is and who you are, you will recognize the lies you have believed in your life about yourself and about Him that have held you in bondage for so long. You will start to see chains fall off your life. Transformation will take place from the inside out. Abide in Jesus, and you will know the Truth, and the Truth will set you entirely and abundantly free. There is no freedom outside of Jesus. Fix your gaze on Him and be free.

DAY 30

God's Presence Will Go With You

*And he said, "My presence will go with you,
and I will give you rest."*
Exodus 33:14 ESV

God is with you always. His presence never leaves you alone. No matter where you travel, He is there with you. Watching over you and working on your behalf. Wherever He sends you, you will not be alone. You do not have to worry about what you will say or what will happen to you because God will always take excellent care of you. You are never for one moment out of His sight. Do not be afraid. You can rest easy when you know the God of Angel Armies is going before you and behind you and walking beside you. Your life is completely safe in His hands. You have absolutely nothing at all to fear. No one can snatch you out of His hands. He will keep you from harm. Trust God. He is always here.

DAY 31

Never Forget The Good Things

*Let all that I am praise the Lord; may I never forget the
good things he does for me.
He forgives all my sins and heals all my diseases.*
Psalm 103:2-3 NLT

God loves you so very much, and it is His pleasure to fill
your life with good things.

God is your Father, and as your Father, He wants to give
you good gifts. May these gifts always remind you to
praise Him. No one can love you and care for you like God
can. He forgives every single one of your sins. All you
must do is ask once, and it is done. He will never remind
you of them again. He will heal all your diseases. Not just
physical diseases, but emotional, mental, and spiritual
diseases. God is a God of completion. He does not leave
anything in your life untouched by His healing hands. You
can put your life in His hands, every area of your life, and
trust Him to take care of you.

DAY 32

You Are More Valuable Than Birds

Look at the birds. They don't plant or harvest or store food in barns, for your heavenly Father feeds them. And aren't you far more valuable to him than they are?
Matthew 6:26 NLT

Take some time today to look up and observe the birds. They sing songs of praise to God. They gather food, they eat and sleep, and they do not fret one moment. They are not afraid that they will not get food. They are not afraid of not being taken care of. God makes sure they are fed and taken care of daily. What makes you think that He will not take care of you? You are so much more valuable to Him than the birds. You are His prized possession, and He will never leave you in need. Your young will never beg for food. Do not fret; just put your eyes on the birds and remember who your Father is.

DAY 33

God Will Give You Laughter

He will yet fill your mouth with laughing,
And your lips with rejoicing.
Job 8:21 NKJV

Life can be hard sometimes, and it can feel like you have no reason to be joyful but remember in those times that your joy comes only from God. Amidst the most challenging trials, you can still have laughter in your heart when you make God your focus. Rejoice in the struggles because you know that He is in control. You know that even though on the outside things look dark, inside, He is doing a great work. You always have a choice of how you endure trials. You can endure them with joy and laughter and enjoy the journey, or you can travel through them with doubt, worry and fear and be miserable on the journey. It isn't always easy to choose joy, but God will help you if you ask Him. You are never alone on this journey. You can ask God for anything you need. Sometimes you don't have joy and laughter because you haven't asked Him. God loves you, and He loves to see you smile.

DAY 34

Your Shrewd Enemy

The serpent was the shrewdest of all the wild animals the Lord God had made. One day he asked the woman, "Did God really say you must not eat the fruit from any of the trees in the garden?"
Genesis 3:1 NLT

Satan uses the same tactics today to get you to question God's love for you as he did in the garden with Eve. He will whisper to you, "Did God really say?" He wants you to begin to doubt that God has your best interest at heart. He wants you to start to question if God is withholding something good from you. Ultimately, he wants you to walk away from your relationship with God, stay complacent, and forfeit your purpose. Remember, the devil is a liar, and there is NO truth in Him. He does not know how to tell the truth. You can understand that when those questions come that make you doubt God's character, those questions are always from the enemy of your soul. Those thoughts come to steal, kill, and destroy. God is always good, always kind, always loving; He is always out for your good. You can trust in Him and in His promises.

DAY 35

God Binds Up Your Wounds

*He heals the brokenhearted and binds up their
wounds. He determines the number of the stars; he gives
to all of them their names. Great is our Lord, and
abundant in power; his understanding is beyond measure.*
Psalm 147:3-5 ESV

When you are broken and hurting, lean into God. Lay your
head on His chest. He will comfort and protect you. You
don't have to earn anything from Him. He loves you, and
He wants to heal every broken part of you. In His presence
is where you find healing. There is nowhere, and no one in
this world you can run to that can heal you. Run to God.
He is your hiding place. He is your place of safety. His
faithful promises are your armor and protection. Cling to
God. Cling to His love for you. Let Him sing you a lullaby
of His love for you. You are His child. He created you; He
will take care of you. He called you from your mother's
womb. Trust God. There is nothing He cannot do. He flung
the stars into the sky and named them all one by one. His
power is beyond anything you can imagine. He knows
things that you could never begin to comprehend in your
own mind. He will never fail you or abandon you. He is
with you to the end of the ages!

DAY 36

God Never Changes

Jesus Christ is the same yesterday, today, and forever.
Hebrews 13:8 NLT

Just as Jesus never changes, God never change. Jesus came to earth as a representation of who God is. Every single characteristic He has was also God's. God's love and affections for you do not change or waiver according to circumstances or your behavior. God's power never changes. He is and always will be God. He is the Great I am. When everything else around you is shaking and unsteady, God cannot be shaken, He is steady. If you plant your feet on God, He will be your firm and sure foundation. God is the Alpha and the Omega. He was here before it all began, and He will be here when this world passes away. Hold on tight to Him, and you will be safe.

DAY 37

Real Love

This is real love—not that we loved God,
but that he loved us and sent his Son
as a sacrifice to take away our sins.
1 John 4:10 NLT

God's love for you has nothing to do with what you can do for Him and everything to do with what He has already done for you. He sent Jesus to die on a cross for you so that you could be with Him forever. Forever starts now. His love is not like man's love. You cannot earn it or lose it.

God doesn't love you because you love Him. He is the one who initiated this love long before you ever knew Him. God's love is secure, and you can plant your feet in it. It goes beyond your finite understanding. There is no darkness in His love; His love wraps you in light and goodness. It is not according to your behavior. It cannot be measured according to your circumstances. It is the same, always. Never more, never less, but perfect and complete. Love is God's nature. There is no evil intention in Him. God loves you, and He always will love you.

DAY 38

God Is Your Shield

The Lord is my strength and shield. I trust him with all my heart. He helps me, and my heart is filled with joy. I burst out in songs of thanksgiving.
Psalm 28:7 NLT

God is surrounding you on every side. No matter what way your enemy tries to come at you, He is there. Nothing that comes into your life is allowed without it being filtered through God's hands of love first. If it is not for your good and His purpose, He will not allow it. He will give you strength for each thing that comes your way. When you feel like you can't go on another day, God will help you. God will fill your heart with joy and thanksgiving, and He will put His songs of deliverance upon your heart. When the darkness tries to close in, you can lift your voice and begin to feel His joy and His hope arise within you. Singing songs of praise will turn your perspective and your thoughts back to God. Lift up your voice and sing in the darkness. Sing a new song.

DAY 39

All Have Sinned

They kept demanding an answer, so he stood up again and said, "All right, but let the one who has never sinned throw the first stone!" Then he stooped down again and wrote in the dust. When the accusers heard this, they slipped away one by one, beginning with the oldest, until only Jesus was left in the middle of the crowd with the woman. Then Jesus stood up again and said to the woman, "Where are your accusers? Didn't even one of them condemn you?" "No, Lord," she said. And Jesus said, "Neither do I. Go and sin no more."
John 8:7-11 NLT

All have sinned and fallen short of God's glory. You are not the only one who struggles with sin. Only One was completely perfect and completely sin-free who walked the earth, Jesus. You are not Jesus, and I know you will have times of struggle. Remember that when you sin, God does not lay condemnation on you. The world will condemn you, but you do not live by the rules of the world; you live by the rules of God's Kingdom. There is not one person who condemns you that has not sinned at some point themselves. Build your identity and worth on God's view of you, not the world's view of you. You will always be shaky and wavering if you try to please the world. God says you are holy and blameless as you stand before Him because of the blood of Jesus. Now you go and see yourself that way.

DAY 40

Oh, What A Glorious Day

But here on this mountain, God-of-the-Angel-Armies will throw a feast for all the people of the world, A feast of the finest foods, a feast with vintage wines, a feast of seven courses, a feast lavish with gourmet desserts. And here on this mountain, God will banish the pall of doom hanging over all peoples, The shadow of doom darkening all nations. Yes, he'll banish death forever. And God will wipe the tears from every face. He'll remove every sign of disgrace from his people, wherever they are.
Yes! God says so!
Isaiah 25:6-9 MSG

Oh, what a glorious day when you finally see God face-to-face! There we will throw a party, and the have finest of foods, better than any you have ever tasted on earth. There will be rejoicing together and dancing on that day when death has been banished forever. There will be no more tears. No more pain. All the worries and anxieties of this world will be wiped away. Sin will have tempted you for its last time, and you will be home. You will be with all the people who have put their faith in Jesus and endured to the end. Oh, what a glorious, glorious day when Jesus shall reign forever, and our hearts are finally together for eternity.

DAY 41

We Are Going To The Other Side

As evening came, Jesus said to his disciples, "Let's cross
to the other side of the lake."
So they arrived at the other side of the lake,
in the region of the Gerasenes
Mark 4:35; 5:1 NLT

When you are in the middle of your storm and think you are about to sink, remember God's promise to the disciples that they were going to the other side. Don't let the storm in the middle cause you to doubt what God said before you started the journey to the other side. When the waves start breaking over the boat, and you feel like you are sure to sink at any moment, remind yourself that God is faithful, and His promises always prove true. The storm in the middle is just part of the journey. It is in the storm that you will see God's faithfulness. It is in the storm that you will see that He will never leave your side. The storm will pass, and you will arrive safely at the other side. Don't give up in the middle. Don't jump out of the boat. Don't lose sight of Him and be distracted by the noise around you. Just trust. There is so much joy and blessing waiting for you on the other side. There are people that you will minister to when we get there. Just enjoy the journey with God.

DAY 42

Just Believe

Therefore, since we have been made right in God's sight by faith, we have peace with God because of what Jesus Christ our Lord has done for us.
Romans 5:1 NLT

There is nothing you can do to earn righteousness. All your efforts to try to appease God are as filthy rags. All He ask of you is to believe. Believe in Jesus and His finished work at the cross, and instantly you are made righteous before God. He paid the price with His blood so that you wouldn't have to. Freely you receive grace and mercy from God. Your righteousness is sealed in the blood of Jesus. There is nothing you can do to earn it and nothing you must do to keep it. Just trust in God, and trust in His goodness to you. It seems unbelievable, but that's because He does not do things the way the world does things. Just allow yourself to believe and be free.

DAY 43

You Are Carried

"Listen to me, descendants of Jacob, all you who remain in Israel. I have cared for you since you were born. Yes, I carried you before you were born. I will be your God throughout your lifetime— until your hair is white with age. I made you, and I will care for you. I will carry you along and save you.
Isaiah 46:3-4 NLT

Before you were ever born, you were already in God's care. You were already thought of and planned for. He knew you before He created you. He has been your God since before you were born, and He will be your God throughout your lifetime, which means He will carry you along and take care of you. He will protect you, defend you and provide for you. Until the day when your time on earth is done, God will take care of you. He will rescue you and keep you. He will always be right beside you, living this life with you. Any time you need Him just call His name. His ears are always opened to hear you. God loves you and will take care of you.

DAY 44

God Is On Your Side

But when I am afraid, I will put my trust in you. I praise God for what he has promised. I trust in God, so why should I be afraid? What can mere mortals do to me?
Psalm 56:3-4 NLT

When you are afraid, run to God. Turn your eyes upon Him. Trust Him to take perfect care of you. Man has no power over your life. God is the One who gives and the One who takes away. No one can snatch you from His hands. When God is on your side, you have absolutely nothing to fear. His promises are always true, and He is always faithful to fulfill them. When you realize who God is and who you are in Him, you will know that you are safe and that no one and nothing can harm you. There will be praise that fills your heart as you rest your life in God's loving hands. Trust in Him today and know that He is on your side.

DAY 45

Changing Seasons

For behold, the winter is past;
the rain is over and gone.
The flowers appear on the earth,
the time of singing has come,
and the voice of the turtledove
is heard in our land.
Song of Solomon 2:11-12 ESV

Your season is changing. Everything around you has looked like winter. Everything has looked dead and withered, but that season is over for you. When Jesus died, the enemy thought he had won, but not only was there death and burial, but there was a resurrection. The flowers will bloom again, and birds will sing again, and what looked like it was dead is going to have new life. Begin to allow yourself to dream again. This is not the end, it was only a season, and now a new season is beginning. Get ready to see God's plans unfold before your very eyes. You will be amazed at what He is going to do in your life. Just when everything looks hopeless, God breathes in new life. Get ready to live like you have never lived before. This is your season to shine.

DAY 46

Walking Through The Valley

*Even when I walk through the darkest valley I will not be
afraid, for you are close beside me.
Your rod and your staff protect and comfort me.*
Psalm 23:4 NLT

When you are going through what feels like the darkest
time in your life, God will be there with you. God will not
leave your side. He will comfort and protect you. It is in
the darkness that His light shines the brightest. He will
light the way out for you. All He asks you to do is trust
Him completely. Take a step when He tells you to step.
You can know that He will never lead you down a path that
is not for your best. When you emerge from the darkness,
you will be stronger than you have ever been, and your
light will shine brightly for Him. He says let's walk this
dark road together. Entwine your hand in God's, and He
will never let go.

DAY 47

God Surrounds You

But you, O Lord, are a shield around me;
you are my glory, the one who holds my head high. I
cried out to the Lord,
and he answered me from his holy mountain. Interlude
Psalm 3:3-4 NLT

God is always here for you. He surrounds you on every side. He is your shield and your defender. He will call you by name and call you His own. God takes away your shame so you can square your shoulders and hold your head high. You never have to play tiny and be afraid of who God has made you to be. Every time you cry out to God, He hears you. He knows what you need before you even speak your prayer. When God hears your voice, He leans in to listen and immediately goes to work on your behalf. Just give your life completely to Him, and He will take you to heights you never dreamed you would be able to go.

DAY 48

Jesus Gives You Living Water

*Jesus replied, "If you only knew the gift God has for you
and who you are speaking to, you would ask me, and I
would give you living water." Jesus replied, "Anyone who
drinks this water will soon become thirsty again. But those
who drink the water I give will never be thirsty again. It
becomes a fresh, bubbling spring within them, giving them
eternal life."*
John 4:10, 13-14 NLT

Your soul is so thirsty, and you are searching for many things
to try and satisfy this thirst. You have been attempting to
satisfy it with material things, and you have been trying to
fulfill it with other people, but Jesus is the only one who can
satisfy. He gives you Living Water. It becomes a refreshing
spring within you. He not only satisfies you for today but for
eternity. The water Jesus give you becomes a river that
continually flows when you spend time with Him. It causes
dead things to live again. Joy to arise again. It gives life to the
full until it overflows. This Water is free for anyone who
comes. You do not have to earn it. No one can take His Living
Water from you. When this Living Water begins to bubble
up, you can't help but let it overflow out of you. This Water
is like healing oil. It flows over your broken mind and heart
and brings the pieces back together. It cleans out the deepest
of wounds. It softens the hardest of hearts. Come daily, sit
with Him and drink deeply of His Fountain.

DAY 49

Do Not Worry

"If God gives such attention to the appearance of wildflowers—most of which are never even seen—don't you think he'll attend to you, take pride in you, do his best for you? What I'm trying to do here is to get you to relax, to not be so preoccupied with getting, so you can respond to God's giving. People who don't know God and the way he works fuss over these things, but you know both God and how he works. Steep your life in God-reality, God-initiative, God-provisions. Don't worry about missing out. You'll find all your everyday human concerns will be met.
Matthew 6:30-33 MSG

Have you ever seen a field of beautiful wildflowers? Wildflowers grow and flourish in their natural environment without anyone touching them; that's because God takes care of them. He attends to even the wildflowers in the fields, yet even as beautiful as they are, they do not hold a candle to the way He feels about you, His child. You are His masterpiece. He takes pride in you. He loves taking care of you. There is no need for you to be worried and weary trying to figure out how to take care of yourself or think you must be in control of everything because if you don't take care of yourself, no one else will. God knows everything you need before you ask. He is the Creator of everything, and He holds together every single detail. Don't stay frustrated and worried trying to figure out how to make things happen on your own; just give it all to God and trust Him. He will take perfect care of you.

51

DAY 50

Come Out Of Darkness

I will say to the prisoners, 'Come out in freedom,'
and to those in darkness, 'Come into the light.'
They will be my sheep, grazing in green pastures
and on hills that were previously bare.
They will neither hunger nor thirst.
The searing sun will not reach them anymore.
For the Lord in his mercy will lead them;
he will lead them beside cool waters.
And I will make my mountains into level paths for them. The
highways will be raised above the valleys.
Isaiah 49:9-11 NLT

God is your gracious and kind Father. When you hurt, He hurts with you. When you rejoice, He rejoices with you. He loves to defend you and rescue you. God loves to swoop in and be your Hero. God will set you free. He will raise you up and give you a testimony so that you can run to others and help them to find Him. You can declare to them that He will set them free. You will tell how He has taken you from darkness into light. He will raise you up on solid ground, and you will be His voice shouting from the hilltops. God will feed His children, and He will give them Living Water so they will never be hungry or thirsty. God's children will be satisfied with Him. He is a loving, and kind Father and He will lead you and guide you along good paths in life. He will walk beside you through every journey, and God will give you rest.

DAY 51

God Will Never Abandon You

Once I was young, and now I am old. Yet I have never
seen the godly abandoned or their children
begging for bread.
Psalm 37:25 NLT

God always provides for His children. He already knows
your needs before you bring them to Him. God has already
prepared a way to answer your prayers. From the time you
are in your mother's womb until you are old with age, He
will take care of you. He will provide everything you need.
Through the generations of people who fear Him, He will
take care and protect them. Neither you nor your children
or your children's children will be abandoned. God will
bless them and keep them and walk alongside them each
day. Your house will be filled with laughter and joy and
plenty of bread to eat. For a thousand generations, He will
take care of His children who love Him and seek Him.

DAY 52

God Hurts With You

Jesus wept.
John 11:35 ESV

God is not a Father who does not feel emotions with you. He is a kind and gentle Father, and He loves you. When you are hurting, He hurts. He collects your tears in a bottle. He is not unmoved by your pain. God has given you your emotions, and you are made in His image. Jesus wept because He was in every way a man, while at the same time God. He cares about every detail of your life, and if something is important to you, it is important to Him. You can come to Him with every emotion you have, and He will understand. You can cry, scream, laugh, all in His presence. He gave you your emotions, and it is okay to feel them. Just don't let them rule your life.

DAY 53

Do Not Bow Down

Shadrach, Meshach, and Abednego replied, "O Nebuchadnezzar, we do not need to defend ourselves before you. If we are thrown into the blazing furnace, the God whom we serve is able to save us. He will rescue us from your power, Your Majesty. But even if he doesn't, we want to make it clear to you, Your Majesty, that we will never serve your gods or worship the gold statue you have set up.
Daniel 3:16-18 NLT

Shadrach, Meshach, and Abednego knew that even if they were thrown into the fire, and even if they died, it would be better than bowing down to another God. There is no other god like God. He is the only God who is personally involved in the lives of His believers. He comes down to where you are, and He lives life with you. When you put your total trust in Him, He will take care of you no matter the circumstances. There will be times that He will deliver you from the fire. There will be times He will walk with you through the fire. There will be times like Paul you will have to understand that His grace is sufficient in your weakness. No matter what, He is a God who is with you and for you. It is never worth giving up eternity to be satisfied and safe in a moment.

DAY 54

God Carries You

In all their suffering he also suffered,
and he personally rescued them.
In his love and mercy he redeemed them.
He lifted them up and carried them
through all the years.
Isaiah 63:9 NLT

God loves you so much. You are so precious to Him, and He is always here for you when you need Him. All you must do is call His name, and He will run to your rescue. His angels are continually around you and protecting you. When you are tired and weary and feel like you can't go on, God will pick you up and carry you in His gentle, loving arms. He will care for you all the days of your life, and He will care for your family for generations to come. When this life is over, God will see you face-to-face. He will wrap His loving arms around you, and you will dwell in His sweet, sweet presence for eternity.

DAY 55

Jesus Will Snap Your Chains

He led them from the darkness and deepest gloom;
he snapped their chains.
Psalm 107:14 NLT

Imagine being in a dark dungeon locked in chains. There are no windows, and no light is coming in. You can barely see right in front of your face, but suddenly, out of nowhere, you see the light, and moment by moment, the light gets brighter and brighter. You are a little frightened because you don't know who or what is coming toward you, but as the light gets closer, you realize it is Jesus! He has come to rescue you and lead you out. All you must do is speak His name, and suddenly your chains are snapped in half, and you are free. Jesus takes you by the hand, and He leads you step by step out of that dungeon to complete and total freedom. All you must do is call His name, and He will lead you out of any dungeon you are in.

DAY 56

Jesus Gave It All

I am the good shepherd. The good shepherd lays down
his life for the sheep.
John 10:11 ESV

Jesus gave everything for you because He loves you so extravagantly. The Father asked Him to give everything of Himself for you on the cross, and He did. You are never, even for one moment of your life out of His sight. If you look back over your life, you will recognize God's fingerprints. Even in the darkest of times, He was there leading and guiding you in some way. You may not see His face, but you can hear His voice, and you will know His voice. You may not see the path in front of you clearly, but because Jesus is the Light, He lights up the darkness, and you will have enough light to see the step in front of you. He will guide you step by step. Remember that God love you so much, that He gave everything He had for you when He gave Jesus!

DAY 57

God Takes Away Your Shame

I prayed to the Lord, and he answered me. He freed me
from all my fears. Those who look to him for help will be
radiant with joy; no shadow of shame
will darken their faces.
Psalm 34:4-5 NLT

Any time you call on God, day, or night, He hears you.
God leans in to listen to you. God loves to hear your voice.
Every time He hears you, He will answer you. Sometimes,
the answer doesn't come in the way you want it to but
remember He has all knowledge and understanding, and
He sees the end from the beginning when all you can see
is a snapshot of this moment. Ask God, and He will deliver
you from all your fears. Do not be afraid to ask. There are
some things you don't have simply because you haven't
asked. Whenever you choose to look to Him for your help,
instead of trying to do things on your own or looking to
man, He will help you. You will be full of His joy. He will
set you free from all your shame, and His glory will shine
on your face.

DAY 58

You Have Gone From Dark To Light

For he has rescued us from the kingdom of darkness and transferred us into the Kingdom of his dear Son,
Colossians 1:13 NLT

You are God's child. He has redeemed you with the blood of His Son. When you chose to believe in Jesus and live your life for God, in that very moment, you were transferred from the kingdom of darkness where death and sin reign, to the Kingdom of God, the Kingdom of Light, where life and righteousness reign. When you live in God's Kingdom, you will find life like you have never known. It will be a great adventure that you will go on every day, and there will be joy unspeakable and filled with glory. God will blow your mind, and you will experience things you never dreamed you would get to experience. There is so much for you in God's Kingdom. So many dreams to be fulfilled. God will laugh with you, cry with you, dream with you, and watch your destiny unfold. God loves living this life with you.

DAY 59

God's Love Is Steadfast

*For the mountains may move
and the hills disappear, but even then my faithful love
for you will remain. My covenant of blessing will never
be broken," says the LORD, who has mercy on you.*
Isaiah 54:10 NLT

God is so totally enthralled with you, His child. There is
nothing He won't do for you if He knows it is in your very
best interest. You do not have to worry about anything.
Even if the mountains crumble into the sea, and all the
earth is shaken, God will be with you. He will not be
shaken. He will never take His love from you. Even if you
were to walk away from Him, He would never stop loving
you. God's love is steadfast and faithful. It does not change
like the love of man. No matter how far you roam away
from Him, He will never give up on you. God will pursue
you for the rest of your days on this earth. His love and
blessings will chase you down. You mean everything to
God.

DAY 60

Blessed When You Believe

And blessed is she who believed that there would be a
fulfillment of what was spoken to her from the Lord.
Luke 1:45 ESV

It causes God's heart to shout with joy when you believe the promises, He gives to you. It is like when one of your parents promised you something as a child, and you believed they would do what they said they would do. But even earthly parents sometimes must break their promises, but God will never break His promises to you. If He tells you He is going to do something, you can guarantee it will happen. God's promises do not change with your circumstances. Nothing can separate you from Him or His love or promises. Sometimes His promises seem illogical and impossible, but usually, that is how you know they are from Him. God likes to do things that you could never do on your own or even imagine in your wildest dreams. He is the Great I AM! Nothing is impossible for Him. Believe in the small and believe in the big. It is all the same to Him. Just believe, and you will see His goodness in your life.

DAY 61

God Chose You

*But God, being rich in mercy, because of the great love
with which he loved us, even when we were dead in our
trespasses, made us alive together with Christ—by grace,
you have been saved—*
Ephesians 2:4-5 ESV

Before you ever spoke God's name, He knew you. He
chose you. He wanted to show His love and Mercy to you.
You are valuable to Him. He planned for you long before
you were born. God chose to send Jesus to die for you.
Even if there hadn't been anyone else, He still would have
sent Him, because you matter to Him. He chose to do this
freely and graciously, not asking anything from you except
your faith. When you were dead because of your sin, God
made you alive and saved you. It is all by His grace
because He wanted to; it had nothing to do with you
earning it. God chose you; He saved you; He loved you.
You are His precious treasure that He plucked from the
darkness and brought into the light. God would choose you
again every time.

DAY 62

You Have a Future

For I know the plans I have for you," says the Lord.
"They are plans for good and not for disaster, to give you
a future and a hope.
Jeremiah 29:11 NLT

God knows the plans He has for you. He has everything figured out. He knows what He is doing. You do not have to fret or worry over your future. God has a plan to give you the best future you could possibly hope for. His plans for you are good and pleasing and perfect because His will for your life is good and pleasing and perfect. Trust Him with today and tomorrow. There is never any evil in His plan for you. God is good, and God does good continually. You can count on Him to come through for you every single time. Trust Him in the details. He will give you the desires of your heart. God loves you, and God loves watching you walk out the plans He has for you.

DAY 63

In Love God Disciplines

And have you forgotten the encouraging words God spoke to you as his children? He said, "My child, don't make light of the Lord's discipline, and don't give up when he corrects you. For the Lord disciplines those he loves, and he punishes each one he accepts as his child."
Hebrews 12:5-6 NLT

Just as a parent must discipline the child they love; God also will discipline you because He loves you. God's discipline is never hard or harsh. He will never harm you. God is always loving and compassionate, and kind in everything He does, including discipline. Don't lose heart and give up when it seems you are being disciplined; even in this time, He wants you to crawl up in His lap and talk through it with Him and allow Him to comfort you. You can rejoice in God's discipline because just as you would not discipline a child you do not know when God disciplines you, it shows that you are His. God loves you. Never forget that, even during discipline.

DAY 64

Abide In God

Abide in me, and I in you. As the branch cannot bear fruit by itself, unless it abides in the vine, neither can you, unless you abide in me.
John 15:4 ESV

Abide means to dwell, live in, or remain in. You can do nothing apart from God. Human effort accomplishes nothing. You cannot produce fruit by trying your hardest to squeeze fruit out. An apple tree does not strive and strain and get frustrated trying to produce an apple. The tree just effortlessly produces apples. It is the same for you. You cannot do good things and bear fruit by trying to bear fruit. You must abide with God. You make your home in Him, and He makes His home in you. When you are abiding in Him, you will rest. You will not constantly be trying to work something up. Just abide and trust. He will take care of whatever you need as you make your place in Him. When you make God the first thing in your life, everything else will fall into place. You will do things effortlessly for God's Kingdom. Remain in Him, and He will remain in you always.

DAY 65

Do Not Fret In The Middle

Keep a cool head. Stay alert. The Devil is poised to pounce, and would like nothing better than to catch you napping. Keep your guard up. You're not the only ones plunged into these hard times. It's the same with Christians all over the world. So keep a firm grip on the faith. The suffering won't last forever. It won't be long before this generous God who has great plans for us in Christ—eternal and glorious plans they are!—will have you put together and on your feet for good. He gets the last word; yes, he does.
1 Peter 5:8-11 MSG

Do not fret or worry when you are in the middle of a storm because this is precisely what the enemy wants you to do. When you are worried and full of noise in your head, it is harder for you to hear God's voice, so your enemy will roar loud to try and distract you from God. He will tell you that you are alone and that no one understands what you are going through but remember there are Christians everywhere that are going through storms, some may be different than yours, but everyone suffers in some way in this life.

Do not give up on God. This storm will not last forever. The winds and waves will calm again, and you will see clear skies again. Just hold on to God. He will lift you up and place you on solid ground. He will put your back up on your feet again. The enemy does not get to win. God will always have the final say in your life.

Remind yourself that God will work this out for your good and His purposes because He loves you extravagantly.

DAY 66

God Loves To Bless You

*And may the Lord, the God of your ancestors, multiply
you a thousand times more and bless you as he promised!*
Deuteronomy 1:11 NLT

Just as you love to give good gifts to the ones you love;
God loves to give good gifts to you. God loves to bless
you. Yes, life is hard sometimes, but even in the hard stuff,
if you look carefully, you will see His blessings.
Sometimes the biggest blessings come in the smallest of
packages. Don't just look for the big and obvious things
but look for the little things. The smile on a stranger's face
when they pass you. The butterfly that lands in front of
you. The snowflakes that fall so beautifully in the winter.
The laughter with family and friends. The phone call just
to say I am thinking of you. God is in all those things. He
will bless you in so many ways that go unnoticed each
day. Take the time to look and listen. You will see Him,
and hear Him, and feel Him. God is always there, always
whispering and sending you little gifts. Slow down today
and look for Him. Then remember to thank Him for the
small things.

DAY 67

God Is Your Anchor

So God has given both his promise and his oath. These
two things are unchangeable because it is impossible for
God to lie. Therefore, we who have fled to him for refuge
can have great confidence as we hold to the hope that lies
before us. This hope is a strong and trustworthy anchor
for our souls. It leads us through the curtain
into God's inner sanctuary.
Hebrews 1:18-19 NLT

God will never lie to you. If He gives you a promise, that
promise is irrevocable, unchangeable, and unshakeable.
His word is the most solid thing you can stand on. You can
be sure that when you run to God for refuge, you are safe.
You can walk into any situation with confidence when you
have Him as your hope. The hope that He gives you is a
sure and steadfast anchor for your soul. You can have the
confidence to come to Him with any need you have and
know that He is the God of the impossible. What is
impossible for man is nothing for God. He shut the mouths
of lions and split open seas. He raises the dead and call
things into existence that do not exist. He is faithful and
trustworthy. God is loving and kind. When He is your
source, you do not have to fret about tomorrow. God will
take care of everything that concerns you. Lean on Him.
Trust in Him. God is a sure and steadfast anchor for your
soul!

DAY 68

You Are Royalty

But you are not like that, for you are a chosen people.
You are royal priests, a holy nation, God's very own
possession. As a result, you can show others the goodness
of God, for he called you out of the darkness into his
wonderful light.
1 Peter 2:9 NLT

God has chosen you. You are His treasure in the darkness; you are royalty. You have been set apart for His purposes. He has called you out of darkness into His marvelous light so that you can go rescue others from the dark and find more treasures. God wants you to use your voice to proclaim His name to the hurting and lost. Go to the highways and the byways, shout it from the rooftops, whatever it takes to tell those lost in the darkness that there is hope, and that hope is in Jesus. He didn't rescue you to keep it to yourself but share it with others to be a continual river of life. As God feeds you, you feed the hungry, both physically and spiritually. Let your life be a beacon of light and hope to everyone around you.

DAY 69

You Are God's Beloved

And I will lead the blind
in a way that they do not know,
in paths that they have not known
I will guide them. I will turn the darkness before them
into light, the rough places into level ground.
These are the things I do, and I do not forsake them.
Isaiah 42:16 ESV

God will never abandon you. He will walk with you when the road is long and difficult. He will be a lamp to your feet to show you each step you should take. When the road gets to be too hard, God will smooth the way for you. When you need wisdom and understanding, just ask, and He will enlighten you. God will never leave you or forsake you in the middle of your sorrow. He is your kind and loving Father. He will take you by your hand and walk the roads with you. He will show you the paths to take to fulfill the purposes He has for you. Sometimes these paths are not the ones you would choose, but they're the ones that will prepare you for where you are going. Just trust God even when you can't see a way ahead. He will go before you and behind you. God is always with you.

DAY 70

No More Fear In Death

*Because God's children are human beings—made of flesh
and blood—the Son also became flesh and blood. For
only as a human being could he die, and only by dying
could he break the power of the devil, who had the power
of death. Only in this way could he set free all who have
lived their lives as slaves to the fear of dying.*
Hebrews 2:14-15 NLT

Jesus became flesh and blood because you are flesh and
blood. He became a human, so He could die as a human
and break the power of the enemy of your soul, the devil,
who at the time had the power of death. Death no longer
has any hold on your life. God loves you so much and
wanted a relationship with you so badly that He sent His
one and only Son as a baby to become a man and die for
you. Who loves this big? Only a kind and compassionate
Father, only God. Jesus broke the fear of death and gave
you eternal life. When you take your final breath on this
earth, you do not cease to exist; you just go to be with God
forever. You are just a sojourner in this world. This earth
is not your permanent home.

DAY 71

Jesus Is Your Strength & Peace

The Lord gives his people strength.
The Lord blesses them with peace.
Psalm 29:11 NLT

This world pulls and tugs at your heart and mind all day long. The chaos of this world can wear you down physically, mentally, and spiritually. You must remember to take time away from this world and be with God. It is sitting in His presence that you regain your strength and your heart and mind find His peace. Jesus is the Prince of Peace. You can run to many things to try to find this peace, but it is only found in Jesus. You may find a fleeting peace in the world, but only His peace is steadfast and sure. Only His peace goes beyond your understanding. His peace will keep you calm when everything around you is falling apart. He will be your strength. He will be your peace, just run to Jesus.

DAY 72

The Earth Shook

*At that moment, the curtain in the sanctuary of the
Temple was torn in two, from top to bottom. The earth
shook, rocks split apart.*
Matthew 27:51 NLT

The moment Jesus died, the veil that separated you and
God was torn. His blood made way for you to be able to
come to God without fear. Now nothing will ever separate
you from His love for you again. You are now welcome
into His presence. Come freely into the secret place for
communion with Him. God loves to hear your voice and
see your face. The blood of His Son poured down, and
when it hit the ground, the whole earth shook. The rocks
split into as all creation cried out and groaned for the death
of Jesus. Everything in that moment changed for eternity.
God would do it all over again for you, His love.

DAY 73

God's Promises Are Your Armor

He will cover you with his feathers. He will shelter you
with his wings. His faithful promises
are your armor and protection.
Psalm 91:4 NLT

God covers you. As a mother eagle covers her babies in her nest, He covers you with His feathers and shelters you with His wings. He keeps you and protects you from your enemies surrounding you. God whispers His promises to you in the dark of night. You can hold on to those promises when everything starts shaking around you, and the enemy starts firing his darts at you; remember God's promises. His promises are your armor and your protection. The fiery darts of the enemy cannot penetrate through them. When your enemy begins to whisper lies that you will never make it, and you should just give up, you can stand on God's promises knowing that His Word is constant and true, and the enemy is and always will be a liar. God's promises to you are a firm foundation to stand on.

DAY 74

God's Love Is Everlasting

Long ago the Lord said to Israel, "I have loved you, my
people, with an everlasting love. With unfailing love I
have drawn you to myself.
Jeremiah 31:3 NLT

You are so overwhelmingly, extravagantly loved by God.
He will keep saying this to you repeatedly because He
wants you to believe it is true. When you get a revelation
of His love for you, it will change your life forever. God's
love is everlasting. It will stand even to the ends of the
ages. God's love for you is unfailing; it is unshakeable.
There is nothing you can do to earn it and nothing you can
do to lose it. God loves you because He wants to love you.
It is His great pleasure to love you and to pour His love out
on you. He initiated love, and He drew you into Himself
with love. God will never be able to do anything but love.
Love is who He is. You are and always will be His beloved.

DAY 75

It's A New Day

The fig tree ripens its figs, and the vines are in blossom;
they give forth fragrance. Arise, my love,
my beautiful one and come away.
Song of Solomon 2:13 ESV

This is your time to step into the things God has called you to. All along He has been preparing you for something that He has prepared for you. He will resurrect all the dreams you thought were dead around you and bring new life to them. You will begin to see new beginnings all around you. A new season is in bloom for your life. The dead and barren season has passed. Your season of renewal and restoration has begun. The very things you thought were the end for you will be the things that catapult you into your purpose in God's Kingdom. It is time to rise out of the ashes into a beautiful wide-open space with Him. This is your time!

DAY 76

Keep Your Confidence

Therefore do not throw away your confidence,
which has a great reward
Hebrews 10:35 ESV

Do not ever throw away your confidence in God. He is trustworthy and faithful. Even when you cannot see His hand at work in your life, He is working. It is easy to give up when things look dark all around you. Remember that He has taken you out of darkness and set you into the light. The enemy would love for you to throw in the towel right now and forfeit everything I have ahead for you, but the enemy does not get to win. He does not get the last word; God does. Keep your eyes fixed on God and His promises to you. Hold on tightly to them, and they will pull you through the dark times. Remember in the darkness every promise that God gave you when you were in the light. God has a firm grip on you, and He will not let you fall. If you hold on, you will receive a great reward!

DAY 77

Free Indeed

So if the Son sets you free, you will be free indeed.
John 8:36 NIV

Only when Jesus sets you free can you indeed be free. No man or thing on this earth can bring true freedom. You may think you are free, you may feel free for a while, but it will be fleeting. Only Jesus has the key to open your prison doors and break your chains. Your freedom matters to God. He sacrificed Jesus so that you could be free. He is the Way, the Truth, and the Life. When Jesus sets you free, you are not just a little bit free, but you are abundantly free; you are free indeed! Don't let anyone put chains around you again now that Jesus has freed you from them.

DAY 78

Power, Love & A Sound Mind

*For God has not given us a spirit of fear, but of power
and of love and of a sound mind.*
2 Timothy 1:7 NKJV

Fear is never from God. He will never say or do anything
that will cause you to be afraid. If you hear the voice of
fear, you know it is from the enemy of your soul. God gives
you power, the same power that raised Christ from the
dead. God provides you with love, perfect love that casts
out all fear. He gives you a sound mind, you have the mind
of Christ. Any time you are dealing with fear, remember
that there is no room in God's love for fear. As you begin
to understand how much He loves you, fear will be kicked
out of your life. So, when the voice of fear comes knocking
on your thoughts, remember that it is an intruder. It is not
from God.

DAY 79

Seek Him

In those days when you pray, I will listen. If you look for me wholeheartedly, you will find me. I will be found by you," says the Lord. "I will end your captivity and restore your fortunes. I will gather you out of the nations where I sent you and will bring you home again to your own land.
Jeremiah 29:12-14 NLT

When you pray, God listens. When you seek Him with all your heart, you will find Him. God loves to have communion with you. God loves it when you come to Him for your help. It is His pleasure to be with you and answer your prayers. He may not always answer them the way you think He should, but if you trust that He loves you and know what is best for you, you will see that His answers are perfect. He restores your soul and leads you out of captivity when you put your whole trust in Him. He will never fail you or abandon you. He will always be right beside you whenever you need Him. God is your ever-present help. Seek Him with all your heart, and He will be found.

DAY 80

You Are God's Dove

*O my dove, in the clefts of the rock, in the crannies of the
cliff, let me see your face, let me hear your voice,
for your voice is sweet, and your face is lovely.*
Song of Solomon 2:14 ESV

Your face is beautiful to God. You are His beloved, and
He loves to hear your voice in prayer and worship. He
looks at your face, and it is radiant with joy. Your voice to
Him is as sweet as honey on His lips. God hides you in His
secret place far away from your enemies. He holds you in
the palm of His hand, close to His chest. Gods lean in to
listen as He hears the beautiful sound of your voice. Even
a whisper from you causes Him to sit up at attention. You
are the focus of His love. You are always on His mind. He
loves to find ways to lavish you with His love and
kindness. Only you can move His heart. Of all He has
created, all the beautiful wonders of the world, you alone
captivate Him. You are His beloved.

DAY 81

Yes & Amen

For no matter how many promises God has made, they are "Yes" in Christ. And so through him the "Amen" is spoken by us to the glory of God.
2 Corinthians 1:20 NIV

When God gives you a promise, He doesn't expect you to go to work trying to make it happen. He wants you to let it encourage you and provide you with strength and faith. You never have to earn God's promises. Jesus has already paid the price for every promise He will ever make to you. He fulfilled everything needed for you to receive them. All God's promises are yes in Jesus, and all you must do is say, Amen! You cannot do anything to add to what Jesus has already done. His blood was enough. Just receive and stand on the promises, and God will work it all out. God knows what He is doing. His ways are perfect, and all His promises will prove true in due time. Wait patiently as He unfolds it all around you.

DAY 82

God Holds You Close

Even if my father and mother abandon me
the Lord will hold me close.
Psalm 27:10 NLT

God will never, ever abandon you! No matter what you do or how far you try to run, He will pursue you. Even if everyone on this earth turns their back to you, God will not. He is always here for you. He never rejects you or send you away. God loves you, and He always will. You are His prized possession. God picked you up out of the pit, and He will continue to pick you up every time you fall. God will pull you into His chest and hold you close to Him. He is your Father. He doesn't care what anyone else thinks about you or says about you; you will always be His beloved. He will defend you and protect you for the rest of your days.

DAY 83

Springs Of Blessing

*And the Lord will guide you continually
and satisfy your desire in scorched places
and make your bones strong;
and you shall be like a watered garden,
like a spring of water,
whose waters do not fail.*
Isaiah 58:11 ESV

God will never leave you to find your way on your own. He will lead and guide you. He will give you the wisdom to know where to go and what you should do. Come to Him in every situation because each situation will have a new set of directions. God will show you step by step. He will refresh you when you are thirsty and dry. He will strengthen you when you feel like you cannot go another step. God will pour His Spirit out on you, and you will flourish everywhere you put your feet. You will be like a well-watered beautiful garden with an ever-flowing spring of blessing flowing out of you onto everyone around you. Even in your dry season, you will flourish and bloom.

DAY 84

God Is Compassionate

When he saw the crowds, he had compassion on them because they were confused and helpless, like sheep without a shepherd.
Matthew 9:6 NLT

Jesus was full of compassion when He walked the earth; He was a representation of God is. God is full of compassion for you. He doesn't want you to stumble around confused and helpless. He wants you to run to Him. The devil is the author of confusion, but God brings peace and calm. His love calms all your fears. You can trust in God's love for you. His love is like a waterfall continually flowing over you. He wants to heal every broken part of you. If you will hold on to Him and persevere, you will see His goodness in your life while you are in the land of the living. He will not judge you or condemn you. He brings grace and mercy to your life. Let His love flow over you. Let His compassion for you change your perspective of Him. He does not wait to punish you when you do wrong. He longs to envelop you in His loving arms and comfort you. His heart is for your good always. Run to His open arms and let Him help you in your time of need.

DAY 85

Always In His Presence

*Surely goodness and mercy shall follow me
all the days of my life, and I shall dwell in the house of
the Lord forever.*
Psalm 23:6 ESV

You do not have to fear what will happen tomorrow. God already has tomorrow figured out. Even in the next minute He has gone before you. He has planned for every detail of your life. God has planned for you in goodness and in love. All His plans for you are for your good. Every day of your life, you will walk in His blessing. When this life is over, and you see God face-to-face, you will forever be in His presence every moment of every day. God cannot wait to get to spend every moment with you. He can't wait for you to see Him and know Him fully without the separation of heaven and earth.

DAY 86

There Is No Other God

*Where is another God like you, who pardons the guilt of
the remnant, overlooking the sins of his special people?
You will not stay angry with your people forever, because
you delight in showing unfailing love. Once again you
will have compassion on us. You will trample our sins
under your feet and throw them
into the depths of the ocean!*
Micah 7:18-19 NLT

God is God alone. There is no other god besides Him. He
was God from the beginning, and He will be God until the
end. He is the only God who can forgive your sins and
wash you as white as snow. God is not harsh and angry;
He is loving and kind. God is compassionate and involved
in your life personally. He cares about what happens to
you. He is not a distant God, but He is as close as your very
breath. God does not remember your sins; He tosses them
into the sea of forgetfulness, as far as the east is from the
west, never to be remembered again. Forget all the other
so-called gods; He alone is God.

DAY 87

God Waits To Be Good To You

Therefore the Lord waits to be gracious to you,
and therefore he exalts himself to show mercy to you.
For the Lord is a God of justice;
blessed are all those who wait for him.
Isaiah 30:18 ESV

God loves to pour His favor out on you. You are so precious and valuable to Him. He wants you to experience His love for yourself. He wants you to walk this earth knowing that you are so loved. God loves to show you His extravagant, marvelous love in so many ways. God loves to blow your mind with His love. He waits in anticipation to be gracious and kind to you and show you, His mercy. He is faithful to keep His promises always. If He says something will happen, you can take it to the bank; it will happen. It will not be a moment late. God wants you to be enthralled with Him, heart, and soul. He is yours, and you are His. God is completely captivated by you.

DAY 88

God Is The One Thing

*"There is only one thing worth being concerned about.
Mary has discovered it, and it will not
be taken away from her."*
Luke 10:42 NLT

So many voices screaming for your attention all around you every day. Some of those voices are good, and some of those voices are not so good. In the fast-paced world you live in today, it is hard to focus on God. It is hard to be able to sit down and put your complete attention on Him. Martha got aggravated at Mary because she wouldn't help, but Jesus told Martha that Mary was giving her attention to the One thing that mattered, Him. It's okay to let things go sometimes. In fact, it is necessary sometimes because if you don't take time away to be with Him, you will eventually burn yourself out. In the times with Him, you are restored and strengthened to live the life He has called you to live. You can live this life without most things, or at least you can take a break from most things, but you cannot live this life without Jesus. He is the One Thing!

DAY 89

Joy & Gladness

*Those who have been ransomed by the Lord will return.
They will enter Jerusalem singing, crowned with
everlasting joy. Sorrow and mourning will disappear, and
they will be filled with joy and gladness.*
Isaiah 35:10 NLT

God has ransomed you and called you by your name. He
will give you a new song, a song of joy and praise. You
will be crowned with everlasting joy. He will wipe away
every tear from your eyes and turn your morning into
dancing and your sorrow into praise. You will go forth in
joy unspeakable and filled with His glory. He will put
laughter on your lips again. You will enter His courts with
shouts of thanksgiving. When you are consumed with God,
your face will shine with gladness, and His name will
continually be on your lips. He is your God, your
Redeemer, your Deliverer. He is the One who loves you
extravagantly now and forever.

DAY 90

Healing Oil

Your anointing oils are fragrant;
your name is oil poured out;
therefore virgins love you.
Song of Solomon 1:3 ESV

God is your healing oil. It is a fragrance so sweet that He has poured out for you. This oil flows in an ever-flowing fountain. It runs down your brow and over your mind. It covers your heart and your soul and flows down to your feet. Not one inch of you is missed by this healing oil. It washes you whiter than the whitest of snow. This oil flowed from the cross of Jesus. It is the blood of Jesus. There is nothing it cannot touch, and it will always bring healing when it touches it. This oil flows for you, and it never ends. Just step under the flow and allow it to wash over you. You will never be the same again once you have been touched by His healing oil. Let it restore every part of you that has been broken and bruised. It is free to all. Just close your eyes and take a deep breath and feel it flowing right now.

DAY 91

You Are His Focus

How blessed is God! And what a blessing he is! He's the
Father of our Master, Jesus Christ, and takes us to the
high places of blessing in him. Long before he laid down
earth's foundations, he had us in mind, had settled on us
as the focus of his love, to be made whole and holy by his
love. Long, long ago, he decided to adopt us into his
family through Jesus Christ. (What pleasure he took in
planning this!) He wanted us to enter into the celebration
of his lavish gift-giving by the hand of his beloved Son.
Ephesians 1:3-6 MSG

You are the very focus of God's love. Long before He
created anything you can see in this world, long before He
ever laid down the foundations of this world, He thought
of you. God made plans for you. You were already His
prized possession before He ever created you in your
mother's womb. He had you on His mind from the
beginning. God wanted to make you whole and holy in His
love. He wanted to have a relationship with you. God
decided to adopt you as His own child. He took such great
pleasure in making these plans. And now, because of the
blood of Jesus, He takes great pleasure in lavishing you
with His good gifts. You are the center of His attention.
His love for you is over the moon!

DAY 92

God Is Limitless

I am the Lord, your Holy One, Israel's Creator and King.
I am the Lord, who opened a way through the waters,
making a dry path through the sea.
Isaiah 43:15-16 NLT

I AM! God is the One who made everything out of nothing. He is the One who flung the stars into the sky, counted them, and knows them each by name. God is the One who raises the dead and causes the blind to see. He is the One who shuts the mouths of lions and walks with you through fire. He is the One who causes the lame to walk and the deaf to hear. God is the One who causes a barren woman to give birth. He is God, Creator, and King; He is your God. He can do anything that He needs to do for you. There are no boxes you can put Him in, and He has no boundaries. He is in control and sovereign over everything. God answers to no one. Never worry when things look dark because He is your Light. He is all you need Him to be. God is limitless!

DAY 93

God's Love Is Your Light

*Satisfy us each morning with your unfailing love,
so we may sing for joy to the end of our lives.*
Psalm 90:14 NLT

God's love is the light that rises in your darkest of nights.
It is like a refreshing drink of cool water. Just when you
think it is over and you want to give up, His love walks in
the door and turns everything around. Sometimes it feels
like you are walking around in the thickest of fogs and
can't even see in front of you, but the Light comes, and it
breaks the clouds that have blinded you. In God's love, you
begin to hope again. You begin to see life again. At that
moment, you begin to sing again. You sing songs that you
never thought you would sing. Songs of joy and songs of
breakthrough. God's love is the only thing that can satisfy
you. His love is the key that opens the broken parts of your
heart. Let God open your heart today and let the light of
His love in.

DAY 94

Jesus Is The Light

Everything was created through him; nothing—not one thing!—came into being without him. What came into existence was Life, and the Life was Light to live by. The Life-Light blazed out of the darkness; the darkness couldn't put it out.
John 1:3-5 MSG

Jesus was there when everything was created. Not one thing was created without Him. Jesus is the Life, and He is the Light. His light extinguishes all traces of darkness, and darkness will never be able to stop Him. He is breathtaking and majestic. His light can melt the hardest of hearts and shine in the darkest of dungeons. Let this Light envelop you and bring healing and hope to your life. When you walk through the darkest of valleys, this Light will be your guide. It will light your footsteps as you walk. This Light will protect you and keep you. There is no demon in hell that can take this Light from you. Today allow this Light to shine through you!

DAY 95

Nothing Can Separate

*And I am convinced that nothing can ever separate us
from God's love. Neither death nor life, neither angels
nor demons, neither our fears for today nor our worries
about tomorrow—not even the powers of hell can
separate us from God's love. No power in the sky above
or in the earth below—indeed, nothing in all creation will
ever be able to separate us from the love of God that is
revealed in Christ Jesus our Lord.*
Romans 8:38-39 NLT

Nothing in all creation, no demon in hell, nothing good,
nothing bad, NOTHING will ever be able to separate you
from God's love for you. Your worries and fears can't
separate you. Your sins cannot separate you; nothing on
earth or in heaven can separate you from His love for you.
He revealed this love for you in Jesus when He died on the
cross and poured out His blood for you. God loves you
because He wants to love you, and He will always love
you. Even if you turn your face from Him, He will still love
you. He will still pursue you. God's love can break every
chain in your life and knock down any wall. You can count
on His unfailing, unwavering, everlasting love.

DAY 96

He Is Aware

*This poor man cried, and the Lord heard him and saved
him out of all his troubles. The angel of the Lord encamps
around those who fear him, and delivers them*
Psalm 34:6-7 ESV

The very moment you cry out, God hears you. He never
ignores your voice. He is always attentive to your prayers.
He will come and rescue you from your troubles. All you
must do is say His name, and He is there. He is surrounding
you, and He is within you. His angels camp around you
and protect you. They are always on watch for you. He
sends them to deliver you when the enemy is trying to
defeat you. There are times God has protected you and
delivered you from things you were not even aware of.
Even when you are sleeping, He is watching over you. You
can lay down your head and rest in peace, knowing you are
always protected. All throughout your day, God's angels
are standing guard over you. You never have to fear
because He is always aware of you.

DAY 97

Dry Bones Live

Then he said to me, "Prophesy over these bones, and say to them, O dry bones, hear the word of the Lord. Thus says the Lord God to these bones: Behold, I will cause breath to enter you, and you shall live. And I will lay sinews upon you, and will cause flesh to come upon you, and cover you with skin, and put breath in you, and you shall live, and you shall know that I am the Lord."
Ezekiel 37:4-6 ESV

When everything within you feels dry and dead, God speaks life to you. When life is so hard and feels like you can't breathe, He speaks breath into your lungs. When He breathes into you, it will be life to every single cell in your body. His life brings restoration and healing. You will walk in fullness again. The dead and dry parts will be refreshed with Living Water. Only God can do these things in you. Only He can speak life to dead things and see them live again. God is the only one true God, and you will see His power working in your life, and you will know and believe that He is God. Nothing is impossible for Him.

DAY 98

God Is Willing

Suddenly, a man with leprosy approached him and knelt before him. "Lord," the man said, "if you are willing, you can heal me and make me clean." Jesus reached out and touched him. "I am willing," he said. "Be healed!" And instantly the leprosy disappeared.
Matthew 8:2-3 NLT

You can never be too dirty for God. Lepers were exiled away from everyone else because they had a horrible infectious disease, but even this contagious disease did not stop Jesus from touching this man with leprosy. God's love and compassion move Him toward you no matter what the world says about you. He loves you even when you are unclean. God is not afraid of you because He knows He can heal you and make you clean. Your sickness nor your sin keep God from touching you. He will never run from you or reject you; He will always run to you and embrace you. There is nothing that will ever separate you from God's love and grace for you. God can heal you, and He is willing to heal you.

DAY 99

Paths of Righteousness

*He restores my soul. He leads me in paths of
righteousness for his name's sake.*
Psalm 23:3 ESV

When life has left you battle-worn and weary, and
everything within you wants to give up, run to God. He
will bring refreshing and life to you. He will restore your
strength and your soul. God leads you down the right paths
for you. Paths that will take you towards His purposes for
you. God will bring the right people along these paths at
the right time to walk on this journey with you and to
support you when you are tired. God will walk with you,
always giving you wisdom for each step you take. He will
be a bright and shining light to light the way for you. God's
path will always lead you toward Jesus, where your
righteousness is found.

DAY 100

Holy And Blameless

For God in all his fullness was pleased to live in Christ, and through him, God reconciled everything to himself. He made peace with everything in heaven and on earth by means of Christ's blood on the cross. This includes you who were once far away from God. You were his enemies, separated from him by your evil thoughts and actions. Yet now he has reconciled you to himself through the death of Christ in his physical body. As a result, he has brought you into his own presence, and you are holy and blameless as you stand before him without a single fault.
Colossians 1:19-22 NLT

Because of the blood of Jesus, you stand before God right now holy and blameless without a single fault. Everyone has sinned at some point in their lives. No one on this earth is perfect. Jesus was the only person who has ever been entirely perfect and completely without sin. Your sins separated you from God and made you His enemy, but you are no longer separated because of Jesus, the spotless Lamb. The veil was torn, and now you can come boldly into God's presence. You could never be good enough on your own, but because of Jesus, you are completely spotless before Him. There is nothing you can ever do to earn this; it is a gift. Just receive all He has for you. Receive your righteousness by grace.

DAY 101

He Directs You

*The Lord directs the steps of the godly. He delights in
every detail of their lives. Though they stumble, they will
never fall, for the Lord holds them by the hand.*
Psalm 37:23-24 NLT

God loves you, and He cares about what happens to you.
You can trust God with everything that concerns you. He
will guide you and direct each step you take. He will not
show you ten steps down the road, but He will show you
the next step in front of you and then the step after that. On
each step you are on, God will prepare you for the next
step. He delights in taking care of every single detail of
your life. He delights in planning the details. He will
always hold you up, and when you stumble, He will keep
you from falling. God has a firm grip on your life. You can
trust Him with every single moment. He is here for you.
God loves you, and He wants to take perfect and complete
care of you.

DAY 102

God Gave All

"For this is how God loved the world: He gave his one and only Son so that everyone who believes in him will not perish but have eternal life."
John 3:16 NLT

God loves you so very much that He gave His One and Only Son. He did it for you. It was personal. Even if you had been the only one that would ever walk this earth, He still would have sent Jesus for you. You are important to Him. You are valuable to Him. Never doubt your worth in His eyes. This world can make you feel tiny and replaceable, but you are irreplaceable to God. You matter!

He knew everything you would ever do, and yet, He still sent Jesus. You do not get lost in a crowd to Him. He sees you. He knows you, and He cares about you. God is so thrilled that He will get to spend eternity with you. Eternity starts now, here on this earth!

DAY 103

Crowned With Love & Mercy

He redeems me from death and crowns me with love and tender mercies. He fills my life with good things. My youth is renewed like the eagle's!
Psalm 103:4-5 NLT

You are so precious and valuable to God. He sincerely cares about you and wants you to have joy and peace. He wants you to know that you are loved and protected. God gave you your life, and He wants you to enjoy that life. He has redeemed you with the blood of Jesus. You stand before Him blameless. He has wiped all your shame away. He has made you whiter than snow. He crowns your life with love and tender mercies. He lavishes you with good things. He is consistently looking for ways to be good to you. He pours strength and health into your mind and body so that even in your old age, you can be strong and soar like an eagle and fulfill the purposes He has for you.

DAY 104

No More Worry

Do not fret or have any anxiety about anything, but in every circumstance and in everything, by prayer and petition (definite requests), with thanksgiving, continue to make your wants known to God. And God's peace [shall be yours, that tranquil state of a soul assured of its salvation through Christ, and so fearing nothing from God and being content with its earthly lot of whatever sort that is, that peace] which transcends all understanding shall garrison and mount guard over your hearts and minds in Christ Jesus.
Philippians 4:6-7 AMPC

God doesn't want you to worry about anything, come to Him and tell Him about everything. He cares about every single detail that concerns you. There is no detail in your life that is too small for Him to be concerned with or too big for Him to take care of. Turn your worries into prayers and petitions. Be specific in your prayers. Pour your heart out to God. Don't hide anything from Him; He already knows anyway. Leave everything with God and rest, knowing that He is working on your behalf, for your good. When you can leave your worries with God in prayer, then His peace which goes beyond your understanding, will come in and guard your heart and your mind. You will be able to be content no matter what the circumstances around you.

DAY 105

His Eyes Are On You

It's in Christ that we find out who we are and what we are living for. Long before we first heard of Christ and got our hopes up, he had his eye on us, had designs on us for glorious living, part of the overall purpose he is working out in everything and everyone.
Ephesians 1:11-12 MSG

God whispers His love over you. It is He who defines you and gives you your identity. God speaks words of value and worth over you. He provides you with rest and peace. Before you were ever created, He knew you and set you apart as His own. His plan for you is perfect and amazing. You are His beloved. You are chosen, called, and hand-picked. You are God's masterpiece, a work of art. He has something unique for you that only you can do because He knit you together for it. You don't have to try to figure everything out or try to make something happen. God will work out His purposes in you as you are ready. Just fix your eyes on Him and trust His love for you on every single step you take together.

DAY 106

Uncontained Joy

For our heart is glad in him,
because we trust in his holy name.
Let your steadfast love, O Lord, be upon us,
even as we hope in you.
Psalm 33:21-22 ESV

When you truly allow yourself to let go and give everything to God and just rest, you will have peace and joy that will go beyond anything you can comprehend. When you truly trust Him, you will walk with a joy bubbling over to the point that it will spill out onto everyone around you. Those who walk with God in complete trust are satisfied with whatever their circumstances are, and they have joy amidst anything. That kind of joy only comes from knowing how much God loves you and that He will always take care of you. That kind of joy and trust causes a person to wait patiently for God's promises to be fulfilled, knowing they will not be late. When you have that kind of trust in His love and care for you, others around you will notice, and they will want what you have.

DAY 107

A Child Is Born

For to us a child is born, to us a son is given; and the government shall be upon his shoulder, and his name shall be called Wonderful Counselor, Mighty God, Everlasting Father, Prince of Peace.
Isaiah 9:6 ESV

Jesus is the Lord of lords and the King of kings. God sent Him down from heaven to be born as a man so He could save you. So that you could have a relationship with Him. He did this because of His great love for you. There is no one on this earth like Jesus. Jesus, His name is like honey on your lips. It can break every chain. It sends demons to flight. At the name of Jesus every knee will bow! His name is power and majesty. He is Holy and perfect, yet He took upon Himself all your sins and gave you, His righteousness. Jesus, there is just something about that name. God loves His Son more than anyone could comprehend, yet because He loves you also, He sent His Son to die for you so, that sin could no longer separate Him from the one He loves.

DAY 108

You Will Stand

*He is like a tree
planted by streams of water
that yields its fruit in its season,
and its leaf does not wither.
In all that he does, he prospers.*
Psalm 1:3 ESV

When you plant your feet in Christ, you will be standing firm in the middle of the most challenging situations. Your roots will go down deep so that even the winds and the rains cannot harm you. Even amidst ridicule and persecution, you will stand firm. You will bear fruit no matter what season of life you are in because you trust in Him and rely on Him. He will continually pour our His Living Water on you and cause you to flourish and prosper in everything you put your hands to. When others are running around chaotic because of their turmoil, you will be rooted and grounded and steadfast in Christ. When you make Him your place of refuge, you can lay your head down at night and rest even when the storm is howling around you. He is your Secret Place. He is your Strong Tower. He will hold you tight and keep you safe in this life and walk with you into the next.

DAY 109

Your Doubts Don't Scare Me

Now Thomas, one of the twelve, called the Twin, was not with them when Jesus came. So the other disciples told him, "We have seen the Lord." But he said to them, "Unless I see in his hands the mark of the nails, and place my finger into the mark of the nails, and place my hand into his side, I will never believe." Eight days later, his disciples were inside again, and Thomas was with them. Although the doors were locked, Jesus came and stood among them and said, "Peace be with you." Then he said to Thomas, "Put your finger here, and see my hands; and put out your hand, and place it in my side. Do not disbelieve, but believe." Thomas answered him, "My Lord and my God!" Jesus said to him, "Have you believed because you have seen me? Blessed are those who have not seen and yet have believed."
John 20:24-29 ESV

God is not intimidated by your doubts. Your doubts don't scare Him. They don't make Him upset with you. He can handle your doubts about Him or His promises. Your doubts do not change who He is, and they do not change His promises. Even the disciples had doubts. When Thomas doubted, Jesus did not scold him or throw him away; He helped him to believe. Jesus was patient with Thomas and knew what he needed to strengthen his faith.

It is the same with you. God understands you are human, and He knows there will be times you will have doubts.

You will doubt His goodness and His faithfulness. There may even be times you doubt His existence, but that doesn't change who He is or His faithfulness. If you will be honest with God about the doubts and ask Him, He will help you with your faith and strengthen you in your doubts. God will not throw you away or reject you because of them. He will not take away His promises just because you have moments of doubt. He is patient with you through them.

DAY 110

You Are Intricately Made

*You watched me as I was being formed in utter
seclusion, as I was woven together in the dark of the
womb. You saw me before I was born. Every day of my
life was recorded in your book. Every moment was laid
out before a single day had passed.*
Psalm 139:15-16 NLT

You are so wonderful and marvelous to God! He loves to
just watch you. You are His child. You are His work of art.
He remembers watching as He wove each piece of you
together intricately in your mother's womb. From the top
of your head to the tips of your toes, He made you exactly
like He wanted you. You are fearfully and wonderfully
made in His image. He was then and always will be
captivated by you. When no one else even knew you
existed yet, He knew you. He was already enthralled with
you. He beamed from ear to ear as He knit you together
and planned for your life. Every moment was carefully
thought through and planned for. Every detail of every
moment was laid out with the greatest of attention and
care. He wove together a beautiful tapestry for your life
before you ever took one breath. He knew the day you
would arrive, and He knows the day you will join Him
face-to-face. God will walk every day with you on the
journey.

DAY 111

Faith

*Then the frightened woman, trembling at the realization
of what had happened to her, came and fell to her knees
in front of him and told him what she had done. And he
said to her, "Daughter, your faith has made you well. Go
in peace. Your suffering is over."*
Mark 5:33-34 NLT

You never have to be afraid to approach God when you
need help or even when you think you have done
something wrong. Your faith gets His attention. Not faith
in what you can do, or a formula you try to work, but your
faith in Him. Put your faith in Him, in who He is, and His
faithfulness and ability. He doesn't ask you to try to figure
out all the steps on your own or come up with a ritual that
will get Him to answer your prayers. The woman in the
scripture just believed that if she could get to Jesus, she
would be healed. Her faith was in Jesus and nothing else.
This is the kind of faith God is looking for. Doctors and
counselors are good, and God gives them to you to help
you, but ultimately, He is your source. Seek Him, and He
will provide you with the wisdom to know what to do in
every situation. Sometimes, like this woman, it may mean
stepping out and doing something that feels scary, but if
He asks you to do it, He will also equip you to do it. He
will never ask you to do something that will harm you or
go against His character.

DAY 112

Rejoice In Trials

We can rejoice, too, when we run into problems and
trials, for we know that they help us develop endurance.
And endurance develops strength of character, and
character strengthens our confident hope of salvation.
And this hope will not lead to disappointment. For we
know how dearly God loves us, because he has given us
the Holy Spirit to fill our hearts with his love.
Romans 5:3-5 NLT

Don't let the trials and problems of this world cause you
to give up or be discouraged. Know that God is with you
in everything. Let these trials build you and strengthen
you. As you go through one problem and you see Him be
faithful to you in it, it will give you the confidence to go
through the next one. In the middle of these trials, you will
be building character and hope, and endurance. These
things help you to stand when the enemy throws His fiery
darts at you. As you stand, you can also help others stand.
You can go through anything with confidence and hope if
you know how much God loves you. You begin to awaken
to His love as you see Him be good to you and trustworthy.
He has poured His love out into your heart through His
Holy Spirit. He lives in you and is with you in everything.

DAY 113

God Has Heard

The Lord has heard my plea;
the Lord will answer my prayer.
May all my enemies be disgraced and terrified.
May they suddenly turn back in shame.
Psalm 6:9-10 NLT

God is your strong tower. He is your ever-present help in times of trouble. He leans down to listen to your whispers, and He hears all your prayers. He is your great God. There is nothing you can ask that is too big for Him to take care of. He annihilates all your enemies before you. He stands between you and the tormentor, and He fights for you. God, the Greater One, lives inside of you. You have what it takes to do whatever He asks you to do. No demon in hell can stand before you because you carry His Spirit and His strength. All your enemy can do is roar at you, but he has been stripped of his power to hurt you when you are God's child. Do not fear your enemy because God is with you.

DAY 114

He Will Finish His Work

And I am certain that God, who began the good work
within you, will continue his work until it is finally
finished on the day when Christ Jesus returns.
Philippians 1:6 NLT

God will never stop working within you until the day Jesus returns to the earth again. He is a God of completion. He s never start something and leaves it half done. You will not be perfect until the day you are with Him for eternity. He is still working on you and will continue working on you as you look more and more like His Son. You cannot do this work yourself; this is a work only He can do; all He asks you to do is surrender. Yield your whole life to Him and allow Him to do the work in you and through you. You will be amazed at what you see unfold before you as you begin to see changes happen in your life that you never thought could happen. Just keep your eyes on Him and allow Him to do whatever He needs to do, knowing that He will always love you.

DAY 115

You Are Hidden

Keep me as the apple of your eye;
hide me in the shadow of your wings,
Psalm 17:8 ESV

God is your Father, and He will always take perfect care of you. His eyes are always on you like a parent watches over a child. He covers you and protects you as a mother eagle stretches out her wings and protects her babies from harm. You are hidden in Him. When the enemy tries to touch you, he will always encounter God first. He holds you tightly in His embrace, and He will never, ever let you go. His love for you is fierce and will always fight for you and defend you. You never have to be afraid that you will not be protected or taken care of. You never have to try to be in control of everything. God has everything carefully and securely safe in His competent hands. He will take care of you; it is His promise!

DAY 116

There Is Healing In His Wings

*But for you who fear my name, the Sun of Righteousness
will rise with healing in his wings. And you will go free,
leaping with joy like calves let out to pasture.*
Malachi 4:2 NLT

Fearing God's name does not mean you are afraid of God.
Fearing His name simply says you stand in awe of Him.
You give your worship to Him. He is not someone you
should fear. He is not out to get you or hurt you in any way.
God never wants you to shrink back from Him in fear. He
always wants you to run to Him with confidence. He is
holy and majestic, but He is also kind and compassionate,
and wants to help you. God is your healer, and Jesus comes
with healing in His wings for you. He took the stripes on
His back for your healing. There is not one part of your life
that His healing cannot touch. He will heal you and give
you joy that will make you want to dance.

DAY 117

He Will Rescue You

The Lord says, "I will rescue those who love me. I will protect those who trust in my name. When they call on me, I will answer; I will be with them in trouble. I will rescue and honor them. I will reward them with a long life and give them my salvation."
Psalm 91:14-16 NLT

You can rest in God. He loves you more than you can imagine, and He sees your love for Him. God will take care of you. His presence will always be with you. God will always respond to your cries for help. He will show you His deliverance. You will experience His goodness and His Mercy. Because you keep your eyes on Him, He will show you things you never dreamed you would see. God will whisper His secrets to you. God will be your firm foundation. You can count on His love for you every moment. He will satisfy you with life; life more abundant than you could dream of. He will bless you and your family generation after generation.

DAY 118

It Pleases God To Give You the Kingdom

"Fear not, little flock, for it is your Father's good pleasure to give you the kingdom.
Luke 12:32 ESV

God does not want you to live in fear all the time. Fear is a thief. It will lie to you, paralyze you, and make you believe that God doesn't love you, so you must care for yourself. Fear will cause you to make decisions that aren't good for you. God loves you, and He wants nothing but good things for you. His will for you is good. His plans for you are good. It brings Him pleasure when you run to Him and ask Him for what you need. You can ask God for anything. There is no prayer too big or too small for Him to hear. Just as a parent wants to bless a child, God wants to bless you. He wants to care for you. He wants you to involve Him in every single detail of your life every single day. Watch for His goodness in your life in the little things and the big things. If you open your eyes, you will see He is always there. Constantly wooing you and protecting you. God loves you.

DAY 119

Your Protection

The Lord himself watches over you! The Lord stands beside you as your protective shade. The sun will not harm you by day, nor the moon at night.
Psalm 121:5-6 NLT

You are God's child, and He is your Father. He will never abandon your side. He is constantly watching over you. God goes before you and behind you, and He surrounds you on all sides. God keeps you from the harm of your enemy. He is loving and kind. He will not let your enemy overtake you. He puts angels all around you to hold you up and guard your way. God never closes His eyes for a moment. He doesn't miss anything in your life. You are never forgotten or unseen. You are valuable and irreplaceable, and God would do anything for you. Never feel like you don't matter. You matter more than you could ever imagine!

DAY 120

God Declares The End from The Beginning

Remember the things I have done in the past.
For I alone am God! I am God, and there is none like
me. Only I can tell you the future
before it even happens. Everything I plan will come to
pass, for I do whatever I wish.
Isaiah 46:9-10 NLT

There is no other god besides the one true God. He has been doing miracles since the beginning, and He is still a miracle-working God. His power never changes. He does not change. He is steady and consistent. He tells you what will happen before it even happens. When all you can see is this moment, He can see the whole picture. He knows the plan He has for your life. It is a good plan, and He will see it through to the end. God's Word is trustworthy and true. If He makes a promise, you can count on that promise to be fulfilled every time. No one else can do the things that He can do. No one can love you like God loves you or care for you like He does. God will not let you down. He is the Great I AM! And He is enthralled with you! He is the Alpha and the Omega; He is the Author and Finisher of your faith.

DAY 121

Jesus Has Overcome

*These things I have spoken to you, that in Me you may
have peace. In the world, you will have tribulation; but be
of good cheer, I have overcome the world."*
John 16:33 NKJV

When your whole life is shaken, when everything is broken
and falls apart, you can still have peace because Jesus is
greater than all of that, and He overcame this world. He
gives you, His peace. A peace that goes beyond anything
this world can provide you, and peace that goes beyond
anything you can comprehend. God never promised this
life would be easy or that there would never be struggles,
but He has promised that He will never leave you or
forsake you and that He will walk with you and give you
peace through the struggles. So, no matter what is
happening around you, you can be of good cheer. You can
have joy when the world says you should be falling apart.
You are in this world, but you are not of it, and you do not
have to be afraid of the things this world is afraid of. God
is protecting you.

DAY 122

He Carries You Close To His Heart

He will feed his flock like a shepherd.
He will carry the lambs in his arms,
holding them close to his heart.
He will gently lead the mother sheep with their young.
Isaiah 40:11 NLT

You are so precious to God. He wants to always show you that He is gentle and kind and will take perfect care of you. Will you give Him everything? Will you trust Him with every detail of your life? He wants you to know that you can. He intends no harm toward you. He is only ever good and has no darkness in Him. He is not who some have said He is. God is not waiting to punish you every time you make a mistake. He loves you tenderly and wants to pour His love into your life. He will carry you when you are weak. He will hold you close to His heart so the sound of His heartbeat will quiet and calm your fears. You are His child, and He wants to assure you of His care for you.

DAY 123

Wait For God

Yet I am confident I will see the Lord's goodness while I am here in the land of the living.
Wait patiently for the Lord. Be brave and courageous.
Yes, wait patiently for the Lord.
Psalm 27:13-14 NLT

Put your confidence in God, and you will see all that He has planned for you come to pass. Wait patiently for Him. Do not throw away your faith in the middle. He will fulfill all His promises to you. Be brave and courageous when the enemy starts roaring in your ear that you will never make it and that you might as well give up. Let God's promises be louder than his roar. Hold on tight to God, and you will not be disappointed. He will do all He promised He would do. Just be patient, and at the right time, you will see His goodness right here before your very eyes. Trust that Gods know exactly what He is doing and that His ways are higher and better than yours.

DAY 124

You Are Marvelous

Thank you for making me so wonderfully complex! Your workmanship is marvelous—how well I know it.
Psalm 139:14 NLT

God has made you marvelously. You are His masterpiece. Don't ever let anyone change who He has made you to be. He knit you together in His image, exactly like He wanted you from your head to your toes. You were not an accident. God wanted you and made you on purpose for a purpose. Every piece of you is lovely to Him! You are His prized possession. You are a treasure woven together in the dark of the womb! He loves you extravagantly. You are His priority. God will always be here for you. God will always love you. He wants you to understand how valuable you are. No man can take away your value or your identity because He alone gives those to you.

DAY 125

Comfort In Troubles

He comforts us in all our troubles so that we can comfort others. When they are troubled, we will be able to give them the same comfort God has given us.
2 Corinthians 1:4 NLT

When you go through troubles and sorrows, God will bring you comfort. He will hold you close to Himself and calm all your fears with His love. He will pull you into His secret place and spend time with you. He will wrap His loving arms around you and hold you tight. God will walk the rugged paths with you and be your light for each step of the way. God will lead you out to wide-open spaces. He will do this for you, and when you have made it through, He will send you back in to comfort others and lead them to Him, so that He can also lead them out. It will never be up to you to deliver them but to walk beside them and guide them to Jesus so that He can deliver them. God will give you His heart of compassion for those who are walking the same path you walked. You will be a beacon of light and hope for them as you abide in Him.

DAY 126

God's Masterpiece

*For we are God's masterpiece. He has created us anew
in Christ Jesus, so we can do the good things he planned
for us long ago.*
Ephesians 2:10 NLT

You are so amazing to God. You are His masterpiece. He
knit you together bit by bit in your mother's womb. He
intricately crafted every part of you exactly like He wanted
it to be. God shaped you and formed you and prepared for
you long before you knew who He was. God planned for
you long before He even created the foundations of the
earth. He drew you to Himself and introduced you to Jesus
so that you could be born again into His family. God has
nothing but good things planned for you. There may be bad
days, but in the end, He will work everything out for your
good and His purposes. You stand before the world as a
magnificent piece of art on display for God's Kingdom.

DAY 127

His Plans Prevail

The Lord of hosts has sworn:
"As I have planned, so shall it be,
and as I have purposed,
so shall it stand,
Isaiah 14:24 ESV

God has a blueprint for your life. He made this blueprint before you were born. In His plans for you, He considered every decision you would ever make, and He crafted His blueprint around those decisions to get you to the point of finding His purpose for your life. His purposes stand even in the middle of your bad decisions. He gives you free will to make those decisions, but He prepares for those decisions in His wisdom. In the end, it will be His plans and His purposes for you and for His Kingdom that will prevail. Do not lose heart if you make a bad decision. It does not disqualify you from God's promises. Just pick yourself up and walk again. He will redirect you.

DAY 128

It is Finished

When he had received the drink, Jesus said, "It is finished." With that, he bowed his head and gave up his spirit.
John 19:30 NIV

It is finished! Jesus did everything that needed to be completed for you to have a relationship with God. Now there is nothing left for you to do except rest in what He has finished. Don't struggle and strive and be frustrated all the time trying to fix everything yourself and make yourself qualified. You are qualified! He loves you. You cannot earn anything. Jesus's sacrifice was enough. All God's promises are yes and amen in Jesus. Jesus let you know that all was made right between you and God with His final breath. When you accepted Jesus into your life, you were made whole and pure again. Your spirit was washed whiter than snow by His blood that was poured out for you. When the enemy starts asking you what you will do, tell Him nothing because it is finished!

DAY 129

Taste & See

*Taste and see that the Lord is good. Oh, the joys of those
who take refuge in him!*
Psalm 34:8 NLT

Come to Jesus and taste and see that He is good. He will
satisfy you more than the finest of foods. Once you come
to know Him, you will never hunger for anything else.
Jesus will become the One thing you need. He is the only
thing that will fill the hole that you are searching
everywhere to get filled. His love is a love like no other.
Jesus gives you joy like you have never known when you
take refuge in Him. You will never be thirsty again because
He gives you Living Water that springs up as a fountain
that never runs dry. No one and nothing can satisfy your
soul like Jesus. Taste and see that He is good.

DAY 130

You Are Complete

*So you also are complete through your union with Christ,
who is the head over every ruler and authority.*
Colossians 2:10 NLT

When you come to a relationship with God through Jesus,
you are made complete. There is nothing in this world that
can complete you. You already have everything you need
in Jesus. He is your Rock and your Strong Tower. He is
your safe person. Jesus is the One who watches over you
and helps you in your time of need. He is your Provider
and your Healer. He is always with you. He is unlimited.
Jesus can do anything He wants or needs to do to take care
of you. No one on earth can love you and care for you like
Jesus can. You do not need a person or thing to complete
you. You are complete right now in Him!

DAY 131

God Will Equip You

Now may the God of peace— who brought up from the dead our Lord Jesus the great Shepherd of the sheep, and ratified an eternal covenant with his blood—may he equip you with all you need for doing his will. May he produce in you, through the power of Jesus Christ, every good thing that is pleasing to him. All glory to him forever and ever! Amen.
Hebrews 13:20-21 NLT

God will equip you with everything you need to do what He has called you to do. His will and plan for your life are good, pleasing, and perfect. You cannot do anything in your own human strength and effort, but when you rely on Him and trust in Him to do through you what you cannot do on your own, He will work in you and through you powerfully. People around you will know that it is His power and Spirit working in you, and they will also put their trust in Him. He will make your life a testimony of His love and goodness to those who believe in Him. Remember that the same Spirit that raised Christ from the dead lives and moves in you.

DAY 132

God Gives You Life

The thief comes only in order to steal and kill and destroy. I came that they may have and enjoy life and have it in abundance (to the full, till it overflows).
John 10:10 AMPC

Your enemy wants to wreak havoc in your life. He has one purpose: to separate you from God. However, when you come to God through Jesus, you do not have to fear the plans of the enemy because Jesus came to give you life. He gives you life more abundant to the full until it overflows out of you onto everyone around you. Not just to live, but to enjoy life. To thrive and flourish in life. The enemy roars loud sometimes, but always remember that the Greater One lives and breathes inside of you, and the enemy can never snatch you out of God's hands. He may try to thwart God's plans for you, but he is already defeated. No weapon formed against you will prosper.

DAY 133

God Is Not Angry

The Lord is compassionate and merciful, slow to get angry, and filled with unfailing love. He will not constantly accuse us, nor remain angry forever.
Psalm 103:8-9 NLT

You may have been told that God is always waiting for you to fall so that He can punish you, but this is not His character. God is kind and compassionate. He is full of mercy and grace. He waits to be good to you. When you fall, He simply helps you back up, dusts you off, and asks you to walk again. God is not constantly accusing you; the enemy of your soul, the devil, is the accuser. He will be the one whispering lies in your ear about how bad you are and how you can never be forgiven, but God does forgive you. He is full of unfailing love for you. When you sin, He wants you to run to Him, not away from Him. He is always waiting with a heart of love and open arms to embrace you.

DAY 134

God's Love Goes Beyond Comprehension

My response is to get down on my knees before the Father, this magnificent Father who parcels out all heaven and earth. I ask him to strengthen you by his Spirit—not a brute strength but a glorious inner strength—that Christ will live in you as you open the door and invite him in. And I ask him that with both feet planted firmly on love, you'll be able to take in with all followers of Jesus the extravagant dimensions of Christ's love. Reach out and experience the breadth! Test its length! Plumb the depths! Rise to the heights! Live full lives, full in the fullness of God.
Ephesians 3:14-19 MSG

God is the magnificent Father of all heaven and all earth. He is the Creator of everything. He has everything He needs to take care of you. He gives you strength in your inner man by His Spirit that lives inside of you. As Jesus lives in your heart and you put your trust in Him, you will begin to experience His life for you. You will know it for yourself. You can plant both of your feet firmly on His love. His love is a steady and firm foundation. God wants you to experience the breadth of it, see how long it is, dive into the depths of it, and rise to the heights of it—this unbelievable, incomprehensible love that He has for you. It goes beyond anything you could come up with in your wildest dreams and imaginations.

It guards you and protects you every moment of your life. It is unwavering and unchangeable. It can never be taken from you. When you experience this love, you will live life with no fears and no worries because you know God will always take care of you.

DAY 135

God Draws You Out

*Then at your command, O Lord, at the blast of your
breath, the bottom of the sea could be seen, and the
foundations of the earth were laid bare. He reached down
from heaven and rescued me;
he drew me out of deep waters.*
Psalm 18:15-16 NLT

God loves you, and He always hear your voice when you
call to Him. There is nothing He won't do for you if He
knows it is what is best for you. His ears are attentive to
your cry. He will shut the mouths of lions for you. He will
open seas for you. He will protect you and keep you. You
are precious to Him. Nothing is impossible for God. He has
unlimited resources at His hands to be able to care for you
and defend you. He will always come through for you in
your time of need. You never have to wonder if He will
show up when you call His name; the answer is yes! God
is always here for you. He will face down any giant for
you. He will give you strength for every enemy you
face. You can count on God!

DAY 136

Set Your Mind On God

If then you were raised with Christ, seek those things which are above, where Christ is, sitting at the right hand of God. Set your mind on things above, not on things on the earth. For you died, and your life is hidden with Christ in God. When Christ, who is our life, appears, then you will also appear with Him in glory.
Colossians 3:1-4 NKJV

Keep your thoughts on God, not on the things of this world. Fix your gaze upon Him and follow His lead. This is a lot easier said than done because there are so many things wanting your attention. Your enemy is constantly seeking to distract you with circumstances and the people around you. Remember you are hidden in Christ, and you live and move and have your being in Him. The things of this earth will pass away, but the things of heaven are eternal. The only relationship that will be left when this earth passes away is your relationship with God. Make Him the one thing you put your attention and time into. Galatians 2:20 says that you live, yet not you, but Christ Who lives in you. You live this life by trusting in Him, not in the things of this world.

DAY 137

God Is Your Life-Giving Light

For you have delivered my soul from death,
yes, my feet from falling,
that I may walk before God
in the light of life.
Psalm 56:13 ESV

You are safe with God. He has a firm grip on you, and He will not let you fall. God is constantly watching over you to keep you from harm. His eyes are never off you. Like a parent stays close to a child, He stays close to you. You are always in His light. Even in the dark, God is your light. His light brings life to your heart and soul. You never have to fear the darkness. He has overcome the darkness, and it cannot extinguish His Light. His Light will light up the path in front of you, so you will know which way to go. His Light envelops you and shines through you, and everyone who sees you knows that you are His. Do not let the darkness shut down your light. Let it shine!

DAY 138

God Turns All Things for Good

You intended to harm me, but God intended it all for good. He brought me to this position so I could save the lives of many people.
Genesis 50:20 NLT

Just as God has a plan for your life, the enemy also has a plan for your life. However, the enemy does not get to win. He will form weapons in your life to try to thwart God's plans for you. He will send people and other things to try to throw you off course, make bad decisions, and get distracted for the purposes God has for you, but all the weapons in the world will not prosper against God's child. What he throws at you to try to defeat you and bring you down, God will turn around for your good and his demise. What he means to bring you low will only end up taking you higher. Many people will see the mighty works God will do in your life, and they will put their faith in Him because of it. Don't let the enemy intimidate you. He loses this war!

DAY 139

God Gives Good Gifts

*"You parents—if your children ask for a loaf of bread, do
you give them a stone instead? Or if they ask for a fish,
do you give them a snake? Of course not! So if you sinful
people know how to give good gifts to your children, how
much more will your heavenly Father give good gifts to
those who ask him.*
Matthew 7:9-11 NLT

Do not be afraid to ask God for the things you need, or
even the things you want. If earthly parents can give you
good gifts, just imagine what God can do for you. He has
all things at His hands that you could possibly need. He
can create something that does not exist out of nothing. He
gave the Israelites food from heaven. He multiplied loaves
and fishes to feed five thousand people. He can take care
of you. Trust Him that He knows what you need and even
loves to give you the desires in your heart that no one else
knows about. It pleases Him to take care of you.

DAY 140

God Has Seen You

I will be glad and rejoice in your unfailing love,
for you have seen my troubles,
and you care about the anguish of my soul.
Psalm 31:7 NLT

God wants you to know that you have not been forgotten by Him. Even if everyone else around you could forget you, He cannot and will not. You are known and seen. Everything around you may feel like it is shaking right now, but hang on to Him, plant your feet in Him. He is a steady foundation. Even amidst your sorrows, your face will be radiant with joy. God will continually pour His love and mercy out on you. He will wash over every part of your heart and mind and bring peace that goes beyond what this world could ever offer you. In the middle of the storm, you can lay down your head and rest, knowing that God has you.

DAY 141

Blessing After Blessing

*From his abundance we have all received one gracious
blessing after another. For the law was given through
Moses, but God's unfailing love and faithfulness came
through Jesus Christ.*
John 1:16-17 NLT

You have been set free from the law, and now you are
found free in Jesus Christ. Because of God's great love for
you, He sent Jesus to die for you and break everything that
separated you. It was on the cross that His unfailing love
was poured out for you. If He was faithful in salvation,
there is not one thing that He will not be faithful in. God
loves to show you His goodness and pour His blessings out
upon your life. God loves to demonstrate His power and
grace through you. Others around you will see His
faithfulness in your life, and they will want what you have.
They will put their faith and trust in God as He shine
through you. When all seems hopeless to them, you will be
the one who will show them where to find their hope. God
is the anchor of hope for the soul.

DAY 142

Your Worship Is Sweet

I bow down toward your holy temple
and give thanks to your name for your steadfast love
and your faithfulness,
for you have exalted above all things
your name and your word.
Psalm 138:2 ESV

God loves to hear your voice lifted in worship to Him. Your worship is as sweet as honey to Him. It moves His heart of love for you when He hears your words and see your knees bowed down to Him. When you worship, all of heaven pays attention. He knows the times you have offered up deep worship, and it was a sacrifice for you because your world was shaking. When you worship, His presence is so near, and His love comes so alive to you. Worship is the ultimate sign of reverence and awe. Worship during battle causes enemies to flee. Worship is not just in a song; worship is the posture of your heart. Even in the most crowded room, you can worship. When you choose the right choice. When you say no to sin. When your life is lived for God's glory, this is worship.

DAY 143

You Know His Voice

The gatekeeper opens the gate for him, and the sheep recognize his voice and come to him. He calls his own sheep by name and leads them out. After he has gathered his own flock, he walks ahead of them, and they follow him because they know his voice. They won't follow a stranger; they will run from him because they don't know his voice."
John 10:3-5 NLT

God loves that you and He have communion together. Every time you sit with Him and listen to His voice, you begin to recognize it more and more. You must know His voice over every other voice, especially the voice of the enemy. When you come to the place that you can distinguish between His promises and the lies of the enemy, you will be able to follow Him. Your life will be steadier because you will not be able to be swayed back and forth. God's voice is always kind and compassionate. Even in discipline, His voice is loving. He will never speak evil or darkness. He will never condemn you. He loves you, and if what you are hearing is contradictory to that fact, you know it is not His voice. Keep your ears attuned to God, and He will lead you everywhere you go.

DAY 144

Showers Of Compassion

The Lord is good to everyone.
He showers compassion on all his creation.
Psalm 145:9 NLT

God is not distant from you. He is close to you. He pulls you into His chest and comforts you. He is tender and kind. He pours out His love and compassion on you. God is not waiting to punish you, but He longs to be good to you. All you must do is say His name, and He is there. He is closer than your next breath. He is in control of all that concerns you. He will never let you down. When you need God, He will be beside you in everything you do and everywhere you go. He is no respecter of persons, but He is good to everyone who calls on Him. He leans in and listens closely to your voice. He is here.

DAY 145

All One

I pray that they will all be one, just as you and I are one—as you are in me, Father, and I am in you. And may they be in us so that the world will believe you sent me.
John 17:21 NLT

God wants you to know that you can be as close to Him as Jesus is. Jesus and the Father are one. You are in Christ, and Christ is in you, which means that you are joined together in union through Jesus's blood. When you walk this earth, not only do you walk as a human, but you walk as someone who carries the Spirit of God in you. When Jesus died and was resurrected, the Holy Spirit came to live with you and in you; because of that, you were joined with God. Now, the Holy Spirit works in you and through you to show the world who He is. It is through you that people will turn to God. Allow His Spirit to shine through you. Allow Him to work through you and touch the lives of everyone around you. When you live a life that points to God, He is glorified in all you do.

DAY 146

Clothe Yourself In Love

So, chosen by God for this new life of love, dress in the wardrobe God picked out for you: compassion, kindness, humility, quiet strength, discipline. Be even-tempered, content with second place, quick to forgive an offense. Forgive as quickly and completely as the Master forgave you. And regardless of what else you put on, wear love. It's your basic, all-purpose garment. Never be without it.
Colossians 3:12-14 MSG

God has loved you with unfailing and everlasting love. God has poured His love into your heart and over your life. Now He wants you to clothe yourself in His love and pour it out onto others around you. Walk this new life you have according to the fruits of the Spirit. Clothe your life in these things instead of the old nature. Walk in God's character. When someone does you wrong, forgive quickly, as He forgives you. Love deeply without needing anything in return. In all things, be kind and compassionate; you never know what someone is going through. Don't let your anger get the best of you, but always keep your cool. Let others go ahead of you, and don't think too highly of yourself. You take care of others as God takes care of you.

DAY 147

Trust God's Love

We know how much God loves us, and we have put our trust in his love. God is love, and all who live in love live in God, and God lives in them.
1 John 4:16 NLT

When you come to believe and know the love God has for you, you will naturally begin to trust Him more and more. You will not trust someone if you do not know they love you and have your best interest at heart. If God did not even spare His own Son for you but gave Him up, then you can trust there is not one thing He would not do for you. You can trust that He will take perfect and complete care of you. You will come to a place in His love where even though everything around you may be falling apart, you will still be at rest with Him. God is love; it is not just what He does; it is who He is. His character is to love you and take care of you. As you live in His love, He lives in you and moves through you. Let go and allow yourself to fall into His arms. You can trust Him.

DAY 148

You Can Sleep In Peace

In peace I will lie down and sleep,
for you alone, O Lord, will keep me safe.
Psalm 4:8 NLT

God is watching over your life every moment of every day and night. There is never a moment when you are out of His sight. You can lay your head down at night and rest peacefully because you know that your Father is the Creator of the universe and the Commander of Angel Armies! You do not need to carry your worries to bed with you or wake up with them in the morning. God is taking care of all that concerns you. He cares about the most minor details. If it concerns you, He wants to help you with it. Just give it all to Him and rest. You never have to be afraid of anything because He is always with you.

DAY 149

Your Advocate

"If you love me, obey my commandments. And I will ask the Father, and he will give you another Advocate, who will never leave you. He is the Holy Spirit, who leads into all truth. The world cannot receive him, because it isn't looking for him and doesn't recognize him. But you know him, because he lives with you now and later will be in you.
John 14:15-17 NLT

God has sent you the Holy Spirit as your Advocate. He will comfort you and walk with you. He is all Truth, and He leads you into all Truth. The world will not recognize Him or receive Him because they do not know God, and because they do not know God, they will not know Him. You can introduce them to Him, and they will see Him living in you and through. You will do signs and wonders because of His Spirit living in you. You will live in peace when the world around you is in chaos, and they will want to know why you have peace. It is that peace that passes understanding. He is the same Spirit that raised Christ from the dead and will raise your life also.

DAY 150

You Will Be Strengthened

*Now may our Lord Jesus Christ himself and God our
Father, who loved us and by his grace gave us eternal
comfort and a wonderful hope, comfort you and
strengthen you in every good thing you do and say.*
2 Thessalonians 2:16-17 NLT

God gives you comfort and strength. When you go through
dark nights of the soul, God will be your light. God will
walk with you through the darkest valleys and rise with
you to the highest mountain tops. God will use your voice
to speak of His name and tell who He is and what He has
done for you. God will walk with you through this journey
of life and guide each footstep. God is a loving and tender
Father, and He will always take care of His children. He
loves you more than you could imagine. No matter what
you do, His grace will always be there to meet you, pick
you up, dust you off, and help you move forward. There is
no distance too far for God to find you. God will always
search for you when you wander. He will never give up on
you. God is patient and gentle with you. Never feel like
you cannot come to God when you fall. He only wants to
be good to you and help you along your way. Instead of
running from God, run to Him today, and He will meet you
there.

DAY 151

Adventure

God is our refuge and strength,
a very present help in trouble. Therefore we will not
fear though the earth gives way,
though the mountains be moved into the heart of the
sea, though its waters roar and foam,
though the mountains tremble at its swelling.
Psalm 46:1-3 ESV

Come with God on an adventure! Run to the mountains and go through the valleys with Him. Walk through green meadows arm and arm and soar over the storms together. Even when the way looks dark ahead of you, God will be your light. When trouble seems to surround you on every side, He is your Refuge. On this adventure with God, you never have to fear. He will fight for you. When the earth beneath your feet is shaking, He will be your firm foundation. If something stands in your way, God will knock it down. You and God will slay giants and cast mountains into the sea. You will see the sick healed and the lame walk. You will see blind eyes open. Your faith will grow as you go along. God is ecstatic about this adventure called life, and He wants you beside Him as He unfolds all the fantastic things that He has prepared for you along the way. Say yes. Yes, is all He needs from you.

DAY 152

Jesus Reveals God

No one has ever seen God. But the unique One, who is himself God, is near to the Father's heart. He has revealed God to us.
John 1:18 NLT

No one has ever seen God, but Jesus reveals Him in who He is. When Jesus walked the earth, He was kind and compassionate. He did not shy away from sinners or those whom others thought were unclean. Jesus walked and dined with those that others tried to stay away from. He was friends with sinners and tax collectors. He didn't come for the healthy, but for the sick. He poured love on the hurting and ashamed. This is who God is. This is God's character. He would leave the 99 to go and rescue the one. He does not shun you when you are hurting or when you have been walking in sin. He draws you to Himself to take away your shame and sorrow. He runs to you; He does not run away from you. God opens His arms wide; He does not close them off to you. No matter what you have done or where you have been, God is here for you. He is waiting to receive you.

DAY 153

God Is Love

Love is patient, love is kind. It does not envy, it does not boast, it is not proud. It does not dishonor others, it is not self-seeking, it is not easily angered, it keeps no record of wrongs. Love does not delight in evil but rejoices with the truth. It always protects, always trusts, always hopes, always perseveres.
1 Corinthians 13:4-7 NIV

God's name and "love" are synonymous in the Bible. God is Love. When you read this scripture of the characteristics of love, you can know that those characteristics also describe who He is. He is patient and kind. He does not envy or boast. He is not prideful. He does not dishonor people. He is not self-seeking or easily angered. God keeps no records of your wrongs. God does not delight in evil; in fact, there is no evil in Him. God always rejoices with the truth. He always protects, always trust, and He always hopes, and always persevere. When you walk with God, and His Spirit lives in you, you will always walk in all these characteristics. God is Love, and He loves you, and His love is in you, and Love is made complete in this union.

DAY 154

The Way Is Open

And so, dear brothers and sisters, we can boldly enter heaven's Most Holy Place because of the blood of Jesus. By his death, Jesus opened a new and life-giving way through the curtain into the Most Holy Place.
Hebrews 10:19-20 NLT

Because of the blood of Jesus, you no longer must fear coming into His presence. You can walk boldly into the throne room in your time of need. You can come confidently and speak to God like you would anyone on earth. God is real, and He will hear you, and He will speak to you. When Jesus drew His last breath, the veil that separated you was torn from top to bottom. Now you are no longer separated. You no longer need a priest to be a mediator for you. God wants to talk to you personally. God wants to hear your voice and see your face. God wants you to join Him in the secret place and pour out your heart to Him. Tell Him your heart's desires and your dreams. Give Him the worries and cares that you carry, and walk away refreshed, restored, and free.

DAY 155

Miracle Working God

Then our mouth was filled with laughter,
and our tongue with shouts of joy;
then they said among the nations,
"The Lord has done great things for them."
The Lord has done great things for us;
we are glad.
Psalm 126:2-3 ESV

God is still a miracle-working God! He has not changed. He can still raise the dead and split the seas. He can calm any storm. God can still heal the sick and cause the blind to see. He can cause limbs to grow where there was not one. There is nothing impossible for God. He wants you to believe for Him to do miracles in your life. He can turn the hearts of stone to flesh. God can pick up all the pieces of your life and make a beautiful work of art. He turns ashes into beauty. He sets the captives free. What do you need? Ask Him. Come to Him knowing that He loves you and He wants to give you good gifts. He wants to fill your life and your heart with joy unspeakable. He will do a mighty work in your life that all will see and know that He is God.

DAY 156

God Gives Every Good Gift

Every good gift and every perfect gift is from above,
coming down from the Father of lights, with whom there
is no variation or shadow due to change. Of his own will
he brought us forth by the word of truth, that we should
be a kind of firstfruits of his creatures.
James 1:17-18 ESV

He is a good Father, and He loves to give good gifts to His children. Anything good, perfect, or pleasing in your life comes from God. There is no good outside of Him. Even those who don't know Him, see Him when they experience good things. He is consistent and steady. You can always count on Him to come through for you. You became part of God's Kingdom when you heard the truth about Jesus, and you believed. Now, you will forever be part of God's family. You are God's prized creation. Nothing in all creation pleases Him and amazes Him like His children. There is no darkness in God; He is only Light, and the darkness cannot take away this Light. God's light guides you along your way as you fulfill the purpose He has called you to. It is all for your good and His glory.

DAY 157

New Mercy Every Morning

The faithful love of the Lord never ends! His mercies
never cease. Great is his faithfulness; his mercies begin
afresh each morning. I say to myself, "The Lord is my
inheritance; therefore, I will hope in him!"
Lamentations 3:22-24 NLT

God's faithfulness never ceases. His mercies are new every
single morning. If you fall, that is okay. God will never
stop loving you and forgiving you. There is no end to His
kindness. You just get back up and try again. There is
always a new day. Forget about yesterday and look to the
future. If you have God, you have hope. Hope keeps you
anchored and strengthens your faith. If you lose hope, you
lose vision for the future. Hope keeps the dreams God has
placed in your heart alive. If you hold on to God, you will
always have hope, and you will always be able to dream.
Hope big! Dream big! Nothing is impossible for God!

DAY 158

Season Of Hope & Expectation

"Yes indeed, it won't be long now." God's Decree.
"Things are going to happen so fast your head will swim,
one thing fast on the heels of the other. You won't be able
to keep up. Everything will be happening at once—and
everywhere you look, blessings! Blessings like wine
pouring off the mountains and hills. I'll make everything
right again for my people Israel: "They'll rebuild their
ruined cities. They'll plant vineyards and drink good
wine. They'll work their gardens and eat fresh
vegetables. And I'll plant them, plant them on their own
land. They'll never again be uprooted from the land I've
given them." God, your God, says so.
Amos 9:13-15 MSG

There is a new season coming for you. A season where everything will begin to fall into place. This is a season of unbelievable hope and expectation. A season when you will see dreams that you thought were dead and buried for good be resurrected and brought to fruition. Family members coming back together, and relationships being rebuilt. God will cause your feet to be planted deep into the soil of His love, and you will not be shaken. God will pour out His blessings on you and your family, and you will walk in divine healing and health. God is the One who calls forth the rain and causes dry and barren land to flow with Living Water again.

This is a season where things you have prayed for will come to pass. Something that should take months, years, or decades will happen quickly. This is a new season for you. Rejoice in God now before you ever see the tangible results come to be.

DAY 159

This Spirit Lives In You

The Spirit of God, who raised Jesus from the dead, lives in you. And just as God raised Christ Jesus from the dead, he will give life to your mortal bodies by this same Spirit living within you.
Romans 8:11 NLT

The very same Spirit that raised Jesus from the dead lives and moves and has His being in you! He brings life to your mortal body, not only in the resurrection to come but also now, right here on this earth. He moves with power in you and around you. When you do things that you have no clue how you did them, that is God's Spirit living and breathing in you. There are gifts that He has placed in you that can only be brought out by the Holy Spirit living in you. Never think that you are not able because God is able in you. It is His Spirit that does the work in you and through you that you could never do on your own. Never count yourself out for anything. If God calls you to it, He will equip you for it. You never have to try to figure it out because it is not by might, nor by power, but by His Spirit that lives in you.

DAY 160

Refreshing Streams

For I will pour water on the thirsty land,
and streams on the dry ground;
I will pour my Spirit upon your offspring,
and my blessing on your descendants.
Isaiah 44:3 ESV

When you are dry and thirsty, call on God, and He will pour out His Living Water on your soul. He gives you water that you cannot get from this world. It is water that heals, refreshes, restores, and brings life. Not only will He pour out this water upon you, but He will pour out this water on your children and your children's children for a thousand generations. God will pour out His blessings upon generation after generation of those who love Him and call on Him for their help. When you rely on Him and trust that He is all you need, not only does it affect you, but it affects those who come after you. You will constantly be refreshed by this water. Those around you who are thirsty will run to this water. This water goes deeper than the deepest of wells. It is a never-ending fountain springing up to eternal life within you.

DAY 161

God's Love Will Chase You Down

I can never be lost to your Spirit!
I can never get away from my God!
Psalm 139:7 TLB

There is nowhere you can go that God is not there. You cannot go so far that God cannot find you. He is present everywhere. He will constantly pursue you, no matter what you have done. God's love will chase you down and bring you back. You never have to hide from His face. He cares about you even when you sin. When you feel alone, and there is no way out of the pit you are in, He will rescue you. He will set your feet on solid ground again. Turn around and run to God, not away from Him. Let Him embrace you in your times of need. Pour out your heart to Him. He sees the hidden corners in your heart that you don't want anyone to see, and He wants to bring His light and life to those places. Open the door and let Him in. He wants to help you. He wants to make beauty out of the broken pieces. Will you trust Him? Will you run to Him? He is not mad at you; He is in love with you.

DAY 162

Watch God's Plans Unfold

O Lord, you are my God;
I will exalt you; I will praise your name,
for you have done wonderful things,
plans formed of old, faithful and sure.
Isaiah 25:1 ESV

He is the God who flung the stars into the sky. He created everything out of nothing. He spoke, and there was light. He formed you in His image. He thought through all His plans for you with love and care before He ever laid down the foundations of the earth. He had every day of your life written down before you ever took your first breath. God has been faithful to you every moment, and He will be faithful to you for ages to come. God will fulfill all the good plans He has for you. Not one of them will be left unfolded. He is the God who was, who is, and who is to come. He has known you and loved you from the beginning, and He will love you until the end of time and into eternity.

DAY 163

Not Today, Devil

*I will exalt you, Lord, for you rescued me. You refused to
let my enemies triumph over me.*
Psalm 30:1 NLT

Your enemy can make a lot of noise and spit out a lot of
nonsense, but you must remember that is all he can do. His
roar is bigger than his bite. He is a defeated foe. Jesus
triumphed over him at the cross. He can play with your
thoughts and make you think he can hurt you, but he
cannot. The devil does not get to win. His time is coming
soon when he will no longer be able to cause you torment
at all. Until then, though, God will guard you, and He will
help you. He gives you the mind of Christ and discernment
to know when what you are hearing is the lies of the
enemy. God puts His peace around you to guard your heart
and your mind. Keep your eyes on Him and praise on your
lips, and when your enemy comes prowling around
looking for someone to devour, just tell him, not today,
devil, not today.

DAY 164

Give God Your Yes

Then the Lord said to Elijah, "Go to the east and hide by Kerith Brook, near where it enters the Jordan River. Drink from the brook and eat what the ravens bring you, for I have commanded them to bring you food." So Elijah did as the Lord told him and camped beside Kerith Brook, east of the Jordan. The ravens brought him bread and meat each morning and evening, and he drank from the brook.
1 Kings 17:2-6 NLT

Sometimes, when God gives you instructions, they seem very illogical to you. Like why would He want Elijah to be fed by ravens? It is more about your yes than about the instructions. Will you follow His lead even when what He tells you to do makes no sense to you? If you give God your yes, even when it makes no sense to you, He will do things in you and through you that you never dreamed possible. Your part is just to be obedient, and He will take care of the results. You will miss so much that He wants you to experience in life if you constantly question why He asks you to do something a certain way. Others around you may even question why you are doing it, but it doesn't matter; God has the final say. Can you imagine what people would have said to Elijah if he had told them he was going to a brook to let ravens feed him? They probably would have thought he was crazy, but he went, ate food from ravens, and was satisfied. Just give God your yes.

DAY 165

God Delivers You

Many are the afflictions of the righteous, but the Lord
delivers him out of them all
Psalm 34:19 ESV

God takes care of you in every situation. He will never leave you to fend for yourself. His love for you compels Him to always rescue you. No matter how you got into a situation, whether of your own fault or by someone else's choices, God will still rescue you. He is a good Father, and every time He hears His child call for help, He will run to them. God's love for you is fierce and protective. You can always trust Him to deliver you from even the darkest of nights. When everything around you looks like there is no hope, you have hope in God. Hold onto that hope; you never know what is around the corner. Things can change for the good in a blink of an eye. God will continue to deliver you until the day you see God face-to-face.

DAY 166

God's Anointing Breaks The Yoke

It shall come to pass in that day
That his burden will be taken away from your shoulder,
And his yoke from your neck, And the yoke will be
destroyed because of the anointing oil.
Isaiah 10:27 NKJV

It is God's anointing in your life that makes a difference. There is not a man on earth that can empower you with anointing. When you encounter His anointing upon your life, it will break every single chain of the enemy. It will lift the burdens of heaviness that you have been carrying. God's anointing is found only in His presence. When you spend time with Him, you will see bondages you have carried for a long time be broken off your life. Things you have tried for years to shake off will suddenly fall to your feet as you encounter His anointing. Don't run after man for anointing, but just go to God. It isn't something that takes a formula or a unique program; it is simply communing with Him and seeking Him above all else.

DAY 167

Be Still

Be still in the presence of the Lord, and wait patiently for him to act. Don't worry about evil people who prosper or fret about their wicked schemes.
Psalm 37:7 NLT

Be still in God's presence. Just let His peace pour over you as you sit in His presence. Let the calm that God's Spirit brings quiet every fear and worry. Don't fret when things are not happening as quickly as you would like. He has a plan, and He is unfolding that plan. His timing is perfect, and all His promises will prove true. Be patient and wait for God to bring it to pass. Don't try to make something happen in your own strength. Keep calm and wait for Him. God will be faithful to do what He said He would do in your life and situation. You can count on God. Don't get frustrated when you see others around you prospering; just wait on God.

DAY 168

Look Up

But now, take another look. I'm going to give this city a thorough renovation, working a true healing inside and out. I'm going to show them life whole, life brimming with blessings. I'll restore everything that was lost to Judah and Jerusalem. I'll build everything back as good as new. I'll scrub them clean from the dirt they've done against me. I'll forgive everything they've done wrong, forgive all their rebellions. And Jerusalem will be a center of joy and praise and glory for all the countries on earth. They'll get reports on all the good I'm doing for her. They'll be in awe of the blessings I am pouring on her.
Jeremiah 33:6-9 MSG

Keep your eyes up and watch what God is about to do for you. Put your eyes on God and make Him your priority, God will restore everything that the enemy has stolen. He will heal you from the inside out. He will give you a whole new way of living and thinking. You will be a trophy of His love and grace. God will pour His love and kindness out on you and your family. Keep Him the center of everything in your life, and you will have the wisdom to make Godly decisions. God will give you joy overflowing and a new song on your lips. He is the God of the impossible, and He will do the impossible for those who love Him and seek Him. Everyone around you will stand with in awe of the wonderous things He will do in your life. Just look up!

DAY 169

A River Of Joy

*A river brings joy to the city of our God, the sacred home
of the Most High. God dwells in that city; it cannot be
destroyed. From the very break of day,
God will protect it.*
Psalm 46:4-5 NLT

When you come, and drink of God, rivers of living water
will flow out of you. It will spring up a well within your
soul. This river brings life more abundant and joy
overflowing. When He is your God, He makes His home
in you. You become His holy temple, His dwelling place.
God will be like a fortified wall around you. He will protect
you and keep you in the days of turmoil. You will be
sustained. God will be your firm and steady foundation. He
will never abandon you or fail you. He will not let your
enemies overtake you. You can trust God with every detail
of your life. He will take excellent care of you always. God
loves you.

DAY 170

Feast In The Darkness

*You prepare a feast for me in the presence of my enemies.
You honor me by anointing my head with oil. My cup
overflows with blessings.*
Psalm 23:5 NLT

Even in the middle of the battle, God will prepare a feast
for you right before your enemies. You will have peace and
calm during all that is shaking around you. Your enemies
will be confused at why you are not fretting and running in
chaos. You will be able to rest in God's love and see His
blessings poured out over you right there amidst the hard
stuff. God will set you up on a steady rock and anoint your
head with oil. What the enemy sent to take you out will be
the very thing that will compel you to your destiny. The
devil does not get to win. Not only will you be blessed, but
when you walk out of the valley of darkness, you will be
blessed to overflowing, better than you even were when
you went in.

DAY 171

Stand Firm

*Christ has set us free to live a free life. So take your
stand! Never again let anyone
put a harness of slavery on you.*
Galatians 5:1 MSG

Jesus took the punishment on the cross for your freedom. He did everything that will ever need to be done once and for all! It is finished. There is nothing left for you to do except believe in the One God sent. You are free because of His blood. The crimson blood that poured down for you and broke every single chain. Take your stand. Stand firm against the lies of the enemy that would try to put a harness of slavery back on you. Walk away and leave it for good. Never let anyone put you in bondage to the very things Jesus died to set you free from. You can't earn it, and you don't deserve it, but God loves you, and His grace is bigger than anything that could entangle you. When the Son sets you free, you are truly free indeed! Guard your freedom!

DAY 172

God Sits You In A Beautiful Place

*You have not handed me over to my enemies
but have set me in a safe place.*
Psalm 31:8 NLT

Your enemy, the devil, has absolutely no power in your life unless you give it to him. God has you covered on every single side. He is with you and in you. He commands His angels concerning you to guard you in all your ways. He opens the seas so you can walk right through them. God sets you free, not just a little bit free, but abundantly free, and He sets you in a wide-open place. He sets you in a position of absolute beauty and peace. Just continue to keep your gaze on Him, your loving and kind Father. God would do anything for you. He always has your best intentions at heart. He is here for you. Just call on Him. When the voice of your enemy begins to become louder, get into the secret place with Him and allow His voice of love and who He says you are drown out all the lies.

You are chosen, forgiven, beloved, beautiful, pure, holy, blameless; you are His absolute favorite. He will always love you with unfailing love, not only you, but also your children and their children to a thousand generations to come.

DAY 173

Blessed When You Trust

*But blessed are those who trust in the Lord and have
made the Lord their hope and confidence.*
Jeremiah 17:7 NLT

When you trust in God, you will be blessed in everything you do. You will be blessed in your coming and in your going. God will bless your relationships. You will be blessed in everything you put your hand to. Your children and their children will be blessed. When you make Him your dwelling place, you will live in the confidence of who you are and Whose you are. You will walk in every circumstance with an anchor of hope for your soul. God will be your great reward. Those who put their trust in Him will never be put to shame. God will honor them and make them a light to shine for everyone around them. Put your trust in God; He will take care of you.

DAY 174

Trustworthy & True

*And he who was seated on the throne said, "Behold, I am
making all things new." Also he said, "Write this down,
for these words are trustworthy and true."*
Revelation 21:5 ESV

When you are in Christ, you are a new creation. Old things
have passed away, and all things become new. You are no
longer who you used to be. That old nature has been buried
with Christ. God doesn't just change things, but He makes
them brand new. Your spirit hasn't just been changed; it
has been made completely new in Christ. Because you are
made brand new, you must now have a new way of
thinking about things. You have now received the mind of
Christ. Think the thoughts that God gives you through His
Holy Spirit. Not only does He make things brand new on
this earth, but also one day soon, there will be a new earth
and a new heaven, and you will get a brand-new immortal
body. You can trust God in these words; He does not just
blow smoke, but His words are trustworthy, and they are
true.

DAY 175

No Other God

You're my King, O God—command victories for Jacob!
With your help we'll wipe out our enemies, in your name
we'll stomp them to dust. I don't trust in weapons; my
sword won't save me—But it's you, you who saved us
from the enemy; you made those who hate us lose face.
All day we parade God's praise—
we thank you by name over and over.
Psalm 44:4-8 MSG

God is the one and only true God. There is no other besides
Him. He is the Lord of lords and King of kings. No enemy
can stand against Him. He is the Commander of Angel
Armies. He gives you the strength to stand against any
enemy. He can cause you to scale any wall. There is no
weapon or army on this earth or in hell that can ever
prosper against Him. God will cause your enemies to fall
before you confused and defeated. You will not even have
to raise a hand against them. His name will be praised
through all the earth. Every knee will bow, and every
tongue will confess that He is God. He is the Alpha and the
Omega, the Beginning, and the End. All creation starts
with Him, and all creation will end with Him. He is the
God of Miracles. He is your God, and He loves you.

DAY 176

God Guides You Safely

*The Lord says, "I will guide you along the best pathway
for your life. I will advise you and watch over you.*
Psalm 32:8 NLT

God is a light to your path and a lamp to your feet. When
you walk with Him, He will show you the way you should
go every time. Keep your eyes on Him. Listen to the sound
of His voice. Keep your eyes straight ahead, and do not
look to the right or to the left. Do not allow the voices that
try to distract you and derail you to get your attention.
Don't try to reason and figure things out in your finite
mind. Do not try to do things on your own, thinking you
know better than God. He knows what is best for you. He
sees things you do not see and know things you do not
know. He knows what is ahead, and He knows how to
protect you from danger. Trust God. He will get you safely
to where you need to be if you let go of control and follow
Him.

DAY 177

God Will Be Your Passion

Place me like a seal over your heart,
like a seal on your arm.
For love is as strong as death,
its jealousy as enduring as the grave.
Love flashes like fire,
the brightest kind of flame.
Song of Songs 8:6 NLT

God will be your all-consuming fire. Make Him the passion of your heart. He will give you His presence, and it will be like a fire shut up in your bones. When God is your passion, you will never be satisfied with anything on this earth. You will set your mind on the things of heaven. Learning to commune with each other. You will learn intimacy with God. He knows you like no one else knows you. He is your living, breathing God. When your passion burns for Him, it will be stronger than any power of darkness. His fire will consume you, and your pursuit for more of Him will be unrelenting. He will show you His glory and shine His light upon your face.

DAY 178

While You Were Still Lost

*But God showed his great love for us by sending Christ to
die for us while we were still sinners.*
Romans 5:8 NLT

Before you ever knew God, before you ever did anything
for Him, while you were still lost and ungodly, He poured
out His love for you. His love for you was made public and
proven on the cross when Jesus died in your place. God
loves you extravagantly and unwaveringly. There is
nothing He wouldn't do for you. You are His child, and
God loves to lavish His love and His blessings upon you.
He is pleased with you and proud of you, not because you
always do everything right or act right, but because you are
His child. He chose you to love. You can count on Him to
take care of you. You can trust God with everything that
concerns you.

DAY 179

His Presence Wraps Around You

With God rests my salvation and my glory; He is my Rock of unyielding strength and impenetrable hardness, and my refuge is in God! Trust in, lean on, rely on, and have confidence in Him at all times, you people; pour out your hearts before Him. God is a refuge for us (a fortress and a high tower). Selah [pause, and calmly think of that]!
Psalm 62:7-8 AMPC

God longs to hear your voice. He loves it when you entwine your heart with His. He cares about everything that happens in your life. He doesn't need you to play games with Him; He wants you to be honest with Him. Tell Him exactly how you feel. It is okay to feel your emotions. Process through them with Him. Tell Him when you are angry, even if you are angry with Him. Tell God when you are hurting or offended. Let Him run to your rescue. Allow Him to be your Hero. God can handle whatever you are going through. Bring it into His throne room and sit in His presence. Let God heal you and comfort you. Let Him wrap His loving arms around you. His presence will envelop you like a sweet caress. You can trust God; He will help you.

DAY 180

Change Is Coming

You will live in joy and peace. The mountains and hills will burst into song, and the trees of the field will clap their hands! Where once there were thorns, cypress trees will grow. Where nettles grew, myrtles will sprout up. These events will bring great honor to the Lord's name; they will be an everlasting sign of his power and love.
Isaiah 55:12-13 NLT

Everything is about to change for you. Where there was so much turmoil and sorrow, there is going to be peace and joy. Where there has been mourning and dead dreams, there will be laughter and new desires being birthed. Your time of waiting is coming to an end. God is making a pathway through your desert. He is opening up riverways through the dry and barren lands. He is doing new things before your very eyes. Everyone who sees these things will know that it is God, the One and only true God, who has done these things for you. It will be a sign of how great and unfailing His love for you is and how nothing can stop His power from working on your behalf. Get ready to step into your new season. It is right around the corner.

DAY 181

The Best Medicine

O Israel, rejoice in your Maker.
O people of Jerusalem, exult in your King.
Praise his name with dancing,
accompanied by tambourine and harp. For
the Lord delights in his people;
he crowns the humble with victory.
Psalm 149:2-4 NLT

God's joy will bring you strength. Joy is medicine to your whole body. Your step is a little lighter when you walk in joy, and nothing can hold you down. God's joy breaks the chains of depression. It wipes away sorrow and fear. His joy is unspeakable and filled with glory. When you walk in God's joy, you will want to dance in the rain and sing a new song of praise to Him. Joy causes you to hope again. It causes you to dream again. Joy causes those around you to want what you have. It brings light to the darkness. God loves to see you full of His joy and fully alive in Him. When you are full of joy, you are beautiful inside and out. It causes your face to glow a little brighter. Joy causes you to step into victory on the inside before you ever see it on the outside. Let a song rise in your heart today and bring a little joy to your soul.

DAY 182

New Life

*This means that anyone who belongs to Christ has
become a new person. The old life is gone;
a new life has begun!*
2 Corinthians 5:17 NLT

When you accepted Christ into your life, you became a
brand-new person. Everything changed. Immediately your
spirit was born again into God's family. The old life you
had is gone and buried with Christ. It was nailed to the
cross with Him. Now you have a brand-new life! You no
longer must live in guilt and shame. Jesus nailed shame to
the cross. He has washed you as white as snow. The
crimson stain that once was on your soul has now been
washed away. You stand before God holy and blameless
without a single fault. He no longer remembers the old
person you were. Now all He see is His child, purified and
whole. Forget those things that are behind you; they don't
define you anymore. Now you have a new identity. Take
off the old nature and put on the new. Walk with your head
held high and your shoulders squared. The weight of
condemnation cannot weigh you down anymore. You are
brand new!

DAY 183

Intricately Woven

*You made all the delicate, inner parts of my body
and knit me together in my mother's womb.*
Psalm 139:13 NLT

God knit you together bit by bit, inside and out. He shaped every single part of you exactly like He wanted it to be. From the color of your hair to the sound of your voice, God created you. He took intricate care in even the tiniest details like your fingerprint. There is no one else like you on this earth, and there never will be. You are His one and only you. God loves you and every single part of you. From the inside to the outside, you are magnificent to God. Like a work of art, a beautiful tapestry, you light up this world. You are valuable and precious, and irreplaceable. Never doubt your worth to God. Never doubt that you matter. Your gifts matter, and your voice matters. This world would not be complete without you.

DAY 184

The Light Of Life

*Jesus spoke to the people once more and said, "I am the
light of the world. If you follow me, you won't have to
walk in darkness, because you will have the light that
leads to life."*
John 8:12 NLT

If you follow Jesus, you will never walk in the darkness.
You will consistently be in the Light. This is Light that no
demon in hell can put out. It is Light that breaks through
even the darkest of night. This Light brings life. Full and
abundant life, like you have never imagined you could
have. A life that is free from fear and full of love. When
you walk in this Light, you will light up the darkness for
others around you. When everyone else is stumbling
around in the dark in fear and chaos, you will have God's
Light and life leading you, and you will walk in peace and
calm. They will want what you have. Don't stay in the
shadows and hide your light; rise and let it shine and point
the way to God.

DAY 185

God Pulls You Close

He does not punish us for all our sins; he does not deal harshly with us, as we deserve. For his unfailing love toward those who fear him is as great as the height of the heavens above the earth. He has removed our sins as far from us as the east is from the west.
Psalm 103:10-12 NLT

God is not a mean God who is waiting to punish you for every wrong move you make. God is kind and compassionate, and He wants to draw you to Himself and shower you with His unfailing love. God does not keep count of all your wrongs, but He throws your sin as far as the east is from the west to be remembered no more. God's love for you is so much greater than your sin. When the world wants to condemn you and count you out, God wants to give you grace and hold you close. God will never shun you. He will never walk away from you. He wants you to run to Him. He stands with arms wide open for you. He is not a dictator; He is a loving Father who wraps His arms around you and pulls you into His chest no matter how far you may walk away.

DAY 186

God Is Here Always

"I will never fail you. I will never abandon you."
Hebrews 13:5 NLT

God is always here for you. He will never ever walk away from you. He will never fail you. You can count on Him to always be here for you and take care of you. He will never abandon you or reject you. He always accepts you into His presence. You do not have to get yourself together or try to be good enough for Him. God loves you. He wants to help you and walk this life with you. He is never mad at you or disappointed in you. You are the apple of His eye. You are His prized possession. You have value and worth no matter what anyone has said to you. No matter what names others have called you, He calls you loved. You are His. You were worth Him giving everything for. He is here for you now and for eternity.

DAY 187

God Is Your Safety

*Though a thousand fall at your side, though ten thousand
are dying around you, these evils will not touch you.*
Psalm 91:7 NLT

God is your place of safety. He is your Strong Tower.
Though chaos is all around you, in Him, you will find rest.
God is your strong and firm foundation. Though the earth
may be shaking and the mountains crumbling into the sea,
you will not fall because God is unshakeable. He hides you
under the shadow of His wings. Do not fear what the world
fears or worry about what they worry about. Though they
are dying all around you, you will be safe in God. Keep
your home in Him, abide in Him, and you will be safe. This
world has no control over you because you are His child;
you are not of this world. No one can snatch you out of
God's loving hands.

DAY 188

Hold Tight

*Let us hold fast the confession of our hope without
wavering, for he who promised is faithful.*
Hebrews 10:23 ESV

Do not lose your hope. Hold on tightly to God's promises.
Let them come from your lips and remind yourself of how
faithful He is. Do not let the enemy toss you back and forth
by his lies that God is not trustworthy or that you did not
hear His voice. Keep your eyes on God. He will do
everything He promised you He would do. He is not a man
that He should lie. He cannot lie. There is no evil in Him.
God wants to help you and take care of you. He is your
ever-present help. Remember what He has said and
remember that He is faithful whenever you begin to lose
your grip on hope. Every word God speaks will come to
pass.

DAY 189

Enduring Love

You are my God, and I will praise you! You are my God, and I will exalt you! Give thanks to the Lord, for he is good! His faithful love endures forever.
Psalm 118:28-29 NLT

God's love for you is forever faithful. His love for you is forever true. It goes past all your failures and all your fears, and it heals the deepest parts of your heart and mind. God's love endures from generation to generation. It is never-ending. It never runs dry. His love never fails. His love believes in you and is patient with you. God's love protects you and comforts you. Love is who He is. You cannot separate Him from His love, and no one can separate you from His love. God loved you before you were ever placed in your mother's womb, and He will love you long after this earth has passed away. God's love is eternal.

DAY 190

Not Even The Smell Of Smoke

*Then the high officers, officials, governors, and advisers
crowded around them and saw that the fire had not
touched them. Not a hair on their heads was singed, and
their clothing was not scorched.
They didn't even smell of smoke!*
Daniel 3:27 NLT

Remember that when you walk through the fire, God is right there in the fire with you. He is in control even of the fire. The fires you walk through will only serve to strengthen you and purify you, but they will not consume you. When you walk through fires with God, others will see that you are different even though you are going through the fire. You are at peace and unafraid. You can stay calm in the fire because you know you do not walk alone. You will not just come out untouched, but you will walk out, not even smelling like smoke. There will not be a trace of evidence of the fire on you, except that the things that bound you are gone.

DAY 191

Good, Pleasing, & Perfect

*Don't copy the behavior and customs of this world, but
let God transform you into a new person by changing the
way you think. Then you will learn to know God's will for
you, which is good and pleasing and perfect.*
Romans 12:2 NLT

Do not be like this world. Do not fear the things they fear
or do the things they do. Surrender your life to God
completely. Let Him transform you into a new person.
Spend time with Him and let His presence transform you
from the inside out. Don't worry about what you should do
and stay frustrated trying to figure everything out all the
time. Don't think the way this world thinks, but let your
thoughts be controlled by the Holy Spirit. Give your heart
and mind to God and rest in Him, knowing you have been
given the mind of Christ. Then you will know His will for
your life. You can trust that His will for you is good,
pleasing, and perfect.

DAY 192

By His Spirit

Then he said to me, "This is the word of the Lord to Zerubbabel: Not by might, nor by power, but by my Spirit, says the Lord of hosts.
Zechariah 4:6 ESV

You are praying for some things that you are trying to bring about in your own strength or reasoning and understanding, but your human effort accomplishes nothing. There are prayers that you are praying that can only be answered by God. Things that can only be done by His Spirit. You cannot try harder or pull yourself up by your bootstraps and make it happen. He is the God of the impossible; He is in control, not you. He knows you feel safe if you feel like you can do something and have some control, but that sense of control is just an illusion. You must trust that God loves you, and He knows what I am doing. What you see as impossible is nothing to God. So, let go of needing to be in control, and just rest and watch God be God.

DAY 193

The Hidden Things

Call to me, and I will answer you, and will tell you great and hidden things that you have not known.
Jeremiah 33:3 ESV

There are things that God wants to reveal to you. He wants to share His secrets with you. Things that are hidden away from the natural world. There are things that you can only know when you seek Him. When you call on Him and make Him your only thing, He will share with you things that would be impossible to know without God having told you. He will unveil things to your Spirit that are hidden from those who do not know Him. Sometimes He will ask you to share these secrets with others, but sometimes these hidden treasures will be just between you and Him. Lean into His voice. Strip away all the distractions and listen carefully. Let Him whisper His heart to you as deep calls out to deep.

DAY 194

Perfect Unity

*I am in them and you are in me. May they experience
such perfect unity that the world will know that you sent
me and that you love them as much as you love me.*
John 17:23 NLT

It probably blows your mind to know that God loves you
as much as He loves Jesus, but it is true. He loves you so
much that He sent Jesus to die on a cross for you. Because
He died and made a way for you to have a relationship with
God, now you can all be in perfect unity together. All
God's fullness lives in Jesus and Jesus lives in you, which
means all God's fullness also lives in you. God's Spirit
lives and breathes in you. He is with you, yet He is also in
you. He surrounds you and protects you. You are one.

DAY 195

Reliable & True

For the word of the Lord holds true,
and we can trust everything he does.
Psalm 33:4 NLT

God is true to every promise He makes to you. You can hold tightly to His promises. God's promises are a solid foundation to plant your feet on. Remember in the valley the promises He gave you on the mountaintop. Every single word that comes forth out of His mouth can be trusted. He will never promise something to you and not do it. You can rely on Him; He will never lie to you. Sometimes He will speak a promise to you right before the storm comes to sustain you in the middle of the storm. When the waves and wind are crashing around you, remember the promises. Don't let the storm take your eyes off Him. The storm will calm, and His promises will be fulfilled.

DAY 196

God Holds Your Destiny

But I trust in you, O Lord; I say, "You are my God."
My times are in your hand; rescue me from the hand of
my enemies and from my persecutors! Make your face
shine on your servant; save me in your steadfast love!
Psalm 31:14-16 ESV

If you only knew how much God cares for you. His love
for you is relentless! In your moments of fear and
desperation, you can trust that He will come through for
you. Run to Him. Cry out to Him. He is always right there
beside you and within you. God holds every moment of
your life in His very capable and trustworthy hands. When
doubt and darkness try to invade your mind and heart, He
will come to your rescue. Just say His name. God is well
able to deliver you. He pours out His grace upon you to
give you the power to do whatever He asks you to do in
each moment. Don't live life worrying about what the
future holds. God has your future in His hands, and you
will be alright! Your life and destiny are safe with God.

DAY 197

Hiding Place

You are my hiding place and my shield;
I hope in Your word.
Psalm 119:114 NKJV

God is your hiding place. He is the place you can run to and find rest and peace when the world becomes too much. He has overcome this world. He has stripped it of its power over you. God is a strong tower for you. You are safe in His secret place. You can crawl up into His lap and pour your heart out to Him when everything hurts so bad. God will speak life to you. He will quiet your fears with His love. God will protect you and comfort you. He will wrap His arms around you and envelop you like a warm, fuzzy blanket. God will speak words of hope to you. You can trust in every word He speaks. Just breathe. You don't have to be strong all the time; just allow God to hold you close. Rest your heart and mind in Him.

DAY 198

You Are His

See what great love the Father has lavished on us, that we should be called children of God! And that is what we are! The reason the world does not know us is that it did not know him.
1 John 3:1 NIV

Wow! How wonderful is it that you are God's child! It makes Him so ecstatic and proud to call you His! He loves to lavish you with His great love for you. God loves to proclaim that you are His, and He is yours. You are a child of the Most High God! He is the One who created everything out of nothing. He is the One that holds everything together by His Word, and you get to call Him Father. The world doesn't recognize who you are because they do not recognize who He is. If they only knew that when you are in their presence, they are in the presence of royalty. Do not hide in the shadows, shrinking away in shame and insecurity; you are God's child, let it be known, and walk with your head held high! You are a masterpiece. You are an expensive treasure with more value than the most valuable of jewels. If you could only see yourself for who you truly are and allow yourself to shine.

DAY 199

Radiant Like The Dawn

*Commit everything you do to the Lord. Trust him, and he
will help you. He will make your innocence radiate like
the dawn, and the justice of your cause will shine
like the noonday sun.*
Psalm 37:5-6 NLT

Gods want to be involved in every detail of your life. He
cares about the little things as well as the big things. Keep
conversation with Him all throughout your day. Ask for
His wisdom in every single decision you must make. God
wants to help you. Trust Him, I know what He is doing. He
has your best interests at heart always. He will cause His
light to shine on you. God will uphold you, and your
innocence and new life will shine as bright as the sunshine
at noon on a summer day. God will defend you. He is
always on your side. Lean on Him, rely on Him, and let
Him be the One who cheers for you. He is so proud of you.

DAY 200

You Are Unforgettable

But Zion said, "The Lord has forsaken me;
my Lord has forgotten me."
"Can a woman forget her nursing child,
that she should have no compassion on the son of her
womb? Even these may forget,
yet I will not forget you. Behold, I have engraved you
on the palms of my hands;
your walls are continually before me.
Isaiah 49:14-16 ESV

You are not forgotten! You will never be forgotten! God loves you, and He constantly has you on his mind. His thoughts about you are so vast, you could never come to the end of them. Even if your mother and earthly father forsake you, God will never, ever forsake you. He is always with you. He will never reject you or fail you. Your name is constantly before Him, on the palm of His hands. He is always concerned with what concerns you. You are seen, and you are known. You are loved beyond your wildest dreams. You may have searched and searched for someone to love you unconditionally, someone who loves you for you without having to wear a mask, but you will not find that person in anyone except God. You are unforgettable and irreplaceable to Him.

DAY 201

God Gives You Inner Strength

The Lord is the strength of his people,
he is the saving refuge of his anointed.
Psalm 28:8 ESV

When you ask God, He will give you mighty inner strength. This strength is not brute strength or physical strength. The inner strength that He gives you comes from His Holy Spirit living in you. This strength comes when you feel like you cannot go on and just want to give up. This is supernatural strength. This strength shows up when you should be crumbling because of your circumstances. You can't find this strength by pulling yourself up by your bootstraps. You only see this strength in letting go and surrender. When you yield everything to Him, He will be your strength, and nothing and no one can overcome His strength. Not only will God strengthen you, but He will protect you and surround you on all sides. He will never leave you to fend for yourself. He will always be your Hero.

DAY 202

Trust God

*But you, Israel: put your trust in God! —trust your
Helper! trust your Ruler! Clan of Aaron, trust in God! —
trust your Helper! trust your Ruler! You who fear God,
trust in God! —trust your Helper! trust your Ruler!*
Psalm 115:9-11 MSG

Put your trust in God! He will help you! There is nothing
that is not under His control. He has unlimited resources at
His disposal. Just because you cannot see how He can do
it doesn't mean He can't. His thoughts are higher than your
thoughts, and His ways are so much higher than you could
even imagine. He can create things out of nothing if He
needs to. He can cause dead things to live. He can put
breath into dry bones and make an army. He is the God of
the impossible. He gave His Son for you. You can trust
God with absolutely every single detail of your life and
your family's lives. Don't try to do His job; let God be
God, and you just rest in Him. He will take care of
everything that concerns you both now and forever.

DAY 203

Punished For You

Surely He has borne our griefs (sicknesses, weaknesses,
and distresses) and carried our sorrows and pains [of
punishment], yet we [ignorantly] considered Him
stricken, smitten, and afflicted by God
[as if with leprosy].
Isaiah 53:4 AMPC

Jesus was born to die for you. He carried all your
sicknesses and diseases, whether physical, mental,
emotional, or spiritual. He did not leave anything
untouched. He endured tormenting and persecution that
should have been yours to endure. People looked at Him
and thought He was being punished because of His own
sins and that God was the one punishing Him, but He did
this all for you. Before He laid down the foundations of the
world, He had a plan that He would come, and He would
take upon Him everything that you should be punished
for. God made this plan because He loves you so much and
wanted to have a relationship with you. God no longer
wanted to be separated from you. He asked His Son to die,
and He agreed, not because you can be good enough to
earn it, but simply because you are so loved.

DAY 204

Hide In God's Love

keep yourselves in the love of God, waiting for the mercy of our Lord Jesus Christ that leads to eternal life.
Jude 1:21 ESV

Hide in God's love for you while you await the end of times. Remind yourself of His love. Rehearse it over and over in your mind. Read about it, sing about it, meditate on it. Let it be the firm foundation that you plant your feet in when this world is topsy turvy and chaotic. It is the one thing that will never change and cannot be shaken or taken away from you. Let your roots grow down deep into it so that when the voices around you are trying to tell you who you are, you will know the Truth. His love will sustain you; it will ground you. You can trust in His love. From today until eternity, His love will never let you down.

DAY 205

Trust Brings Joy

Oh, the joys of those who trust the Lord, who have no confidence in the proud or in those who worship idols.
Psalm 40:4 NLT

When you are trusting God with everything, you can rest. When you are genuinely resting, you will have joy. When you trust in Him, you are not worrying about tomorrow or looking back to yesterday. When you are truly trusting, you can live in the moment you are in and enjoy the life God has given you. Do not put your confidence in anything in this world. Every man is human and can fall. Everything in this world made by man will rust and crumble. When you trust man or manmade things, it is shaking sand, and your house will eventually be washed away.

Only God is truly in control. Only He holds everything together. With one word, He causes nations to crumble and mountains to be tossed into the sea. Keep your trust in God and Him alone. You can trust He will take perfect care of you because God loves you so very much.

DAY 206

Lean Into God

*His left hand is under my head,
and his right hand embraces me!*
Song of Solomon 2:6 ESV

When you are broken and hurting, you can go to God. He will pull you to Himself. He will hold you close to His heart, where you can hear His heartbeat. He will comfort you as a mother comforts a child. His love will wrap around you and envelop you in His warmth and peace. It will be like a blanket around you. When you are wounded, God will care for you. Lean into Him and let go. Just allow yourself to be held in His arms. Let yourself fall into Him and rest yourself in His love for you. He is tender and gentle. He will never scold you or condemn you. He will always soothe you with His words of peace and love. Lay your head on His chest and rest.

DAY 207

Crown Of Creation

When I look at the night sky and see the work of your fingers—the moon and the stars you set in place— what are mere mortals that you should think about them, human beings that you should care for them? Yet you made them only a little lower than God and crowned them with glory and honor.
Psalm 8:3-5 NLT

God is a Holy and Righteous God, yet He leans down to hear your voice. He flung the stars in the sky and made everything out of nothing, yet He loves you more than all other creations. He has made you in His image. You are the crown of all creation. He is thrilled by you. He is enthralled with you. He pours out His grace and mercy upon you. God shows you His glory, and He honors you. You are the apple of His eye. He commands His angels to take care of you. You should never doubt your value and your worth. Nothing can separate you from God's love for you. God loves to spend time with you and see your face.

DAY 208

Your Defender

*And God will provide rest for you who are being
persecuted and also for us when the Lord Jesus appears
from heaven. He will come with his mighty angels, in
flaming fire, bringing judgment on those who don't know
God and on those who refuse to obey the
Good News of our Lord Jesus.*
2 Thessalonians 1:7-8 NLT

God is your defender. He will always be on your side. If
God is for you, who can be against you? He is the God of
Angel Armies. He will fight for you in all things. God's
love for you is fierce. He will always bring justice for you.
Never think you must take care of yourself and defend
yourself. It is better to hold your tongue and let God speak
for you; let Him show up on your behalf. He sees things
you cannot see when you are in the battle; let Him go
before you and prepare the way. He will be a refuge for His
children against the wiles of the wicked. You will walk in
safety under the shadow of His wings.

DAY 209

Protected All Around

*God is bedrock under my feet, the castle in which I live,
my rescuing knight. My God—the high crag where I run
for dear life, hiding behind the boulders, safe in the
granite hideout; My mountaintop refuge, he saves me
from ruthless men. I sing to God the Praise-Lofty, and
find myself safe and saved.*
2 Samuel 22:3-4 MSG

God is your Shelter, your Strong Tower. You can run to
Him for refuge. God will always keep you safe under His
protection. No one can penetrate His walls around you.
God is a strong foundation under your feet; you will not
fall. You can lean on God and know that He is strong
enough to hold you up. You can stand safely on His
mountaintop. You do not have to fear anyone or anything.
When you walk through the journey of life, He surrounds
you on all sides, and He abides inside of you. His wrap-
around presence envelops you. When the enemy shoots his
fiery arrows at you, God's promises will be a shield for
you.

DAY 210

Open Your Hands To Receive

You open your hand; you satisfy the desire
of every living thing.
Psalm 145:16 ESV

When God open His hands, He pours out blessings you cannot contain. He satisfies every desire you have. When you have God, you have everything you will ever need. He wants to open His hands to give, but He also need you to open your hands to receive. To open your hands to receive, you must let go of the tight grip you have on this life. You must give up control and let God be God. Trust that what He has for you is better than you could ever get on your own. He poured down manna from heaven for the Israelites in the desert; He can fill your life with good things.

DAY 211

Now You Have Seen

I had only heard about you before, but now
I have seen you with my own eyes.
Job 42:5 NLT

You can hear people talk about God all day, but it is not the same until you know Him for yourself. He doesn't want you to just hear about Him or just know of Him; God wants you to experience a relationship with Him. He wants you to experience His love, power, and care. God wants you to know Him intimately. You have so much potential inside you and are so valuable, but it is only when you come to know Him for yourself that you can truly know who you are and your value. It is when you come to know Him that you begin too truly live. God gives you a life that is beyond your wildest dreams.

DAY 212

You Hold His Attention

*I love the Lord, because he has heard
my voice and my pleas for mercy.
Because he inclined his ear to me,
therefore I will call on him as long as I live.*
Psalm 116:1-2 ESV

You are so valuable to God. When you need Him, He stops what He is doing, and His attention goes to you. He listens to every single word you say. He hears every single prayer. There is not one prayer that you have prayed or will pray that goes past His ears. Your prayers being answered do not depend on how good you have been today or if you have checked off all the boxes of chores you think you should do for God. He is a good Father who loves His children, and He would never ignore you or reject you. Even before you call, God know the cries of your heart. He leans down from His throne room and answers your prayers. It may not always look the way you want it to, but His ways are perfect, and His timing is perfect.

DAY 213

You Can Count On God

Your steadfast love, O Lord, extends to the heavens,
your faithfulness to the clouds. Your righteousness is
like the mountains of God; your judgments are like the
great deep; man and beast you save, O Lord.
How precious is your steadfast love, O God! The children
of mankind take refuge in the shadow of your wings.
Psalm 36:5-7 ESV

How vast God's love is for you! It is limitless. H would go anywhere to rescue you. He would do anything to help you. It reaches higher than the heavens. There is no greater love than the love He has for His children. He is trustworthy and true to you. His faithfulness is greater than you can imagine, and it goes on for eternity. He is full of wisdom and power, just ask, and He will fill you with these. He is kind and gentle at heart. He is compassionate and tender. God's love for you knows no bounds. His care for you is infinite. He is your Hiding Place. He shelters you daily out of the reach of your enemies under the shadow of His wings.

You can't out love God. You can't out give Him. Even when you are faithless, He is still faithful. It is who He is! He cares for all His creations; not one of them is out of His sight. He is not a harsh God. He wants good for you. He does good for you. You can always count on God.

DAY 214

God's Love Brings Joy

Satisfy us each morning with your unfailing love, so we
may sing for joy to the end of our lives.
Give us gladness in proportion to our former
misery! Replace the evil years with good.
Psalm 90:14-15 NLT

You cannot even begin to fathom how much God loves you. He will tell you over and over because He wants you to know and believe it. When you really believe how much God loves you, you will not be able to help but walk in joy. You will have a pep to your step each day. When bad things come, you know that He will turn those things for good in some way. Life is so much better when you believe that you are loved by God. You can lay down at night and sleep in peace. You can wake up in the morning full of sunshine, even on a rainy day, because His love fills every part of your soul. It is like a light that glows out of every single cell of your body. God's love will sustain you in everything.

DAY 215

This Is The Way

And your ears shall hear a word behind you, saying,
"This is the way, walk in it," when you turn to the right
or when you turn to the left.
Isaiah 30:21 ESV

God will direct your steps. You know His voice, and you hear His voice. When you need direction and don't know which way to go, He will tell you which path to take if you call on Him. If you try to walk this life out all alone, you will have a lot of frustration and struggle. He wants you to ask Him for help. He wants to help you. Sometimes you can't hear His direction because all the voices and noise around you are too loud. You must take time to quiet your mind. Learn to love the silence and sit with Him. It is in the quiet that you will hear His voice speak to you. God will not scream over all the other noise. Listen and look, and you will see His instructions in your life.

DAY 216

You Can Scale A Wall

In his unfailing love, my God will stand with me.
He will let me look down in triumph on all my enemies.
Psalm 59:10 NLT

With God on your side, you can scale any wall; you can
defeat any enemy, not because of who you are, but because
of Who lives inside of you. You live, yet it is not you, but
it is Christ who lives in you. No foe in hell can stand
against Christ in you. You have two things that give you
strength that can get you through any battle, the power of
God's love and the power of His Spirit. The things that
Jesus did as He walked this earth, you can do as God's
Spirit works through you. You can lay hands on the sick
and see them healed. You can cast out demons and set the
captives free. You have all authority over all the power of
the enemy. God is in you, and with you, you have nothing
to fear.

DAY 217

God Goes Before You

*What's more, I am with you, and I will protect you
wherever you go. One day I will bring you back to this
land. I will not leave you until I have finished giving you
everything I have promised you."*
Genesis 28:15 NLT

You will never have to walk this journey alone. God is
always with you, and He will never abandon you. He will
direct your steps and protect you wherever you
go. Wherever you place your feet, you will be blessed. God
is already going before you and preparing things and
people on your behalf. He will finish the work He has
started in you, and He will fulfill every promise that He has
spoken to you. Wait on Him, don't try to go ahead of Him.
Trust His perfect timing. God knows what He is doing. He
had this all planned out before you ever took a breath. This
is not the end of your story, but don't try to make things
happen before you are ready. At the right time, God will
cause everything He has spoken to you to come to pass.
Hold tightly to Him. He will not let you go.

DAY 218

From Tears To Harvest

Restore our fortunes, Lord, as streams renew the desert.
Those who plant in tears will harvest with shouts of joy.
They weep as they go to plant their seed, but they sing as
they return with the harvest.
Psalm 126:4-6 NLT

You have been in a season of mourning and grief. It has been a season of sowing tears and sorrows more than laughter and joy. Your season is changing. The tears you have sown in this season have watered the ground of the seeds God has planted in you, and now those seeds will yield a harvest. You will no longer be discouraged and dismayed, but you will be full of laughter and blessings. What has looked like defeat will turn to victory. What has looked like ashes will turn to beauty. God will cause the things you have been struggling with to become the things that propel you into your purpose. Instead of weeping and sorrow, there will be joy and life. He will cause His river of life to flow over you again and spring up a never-ending well of joy inside your soul. It is time for you to harvest from all the tears you have sown. The things you will take away from this season will be so great you will not even be able to contain them.

DAY 219

Stand Still

But you will not even need to fight. Take your positions;
then stand still and watch the Lord's victory. He is with
you, O people of Judah and Jerusalem. Do not be afraid
or discouraged. Go out against them tomorrow,
for the Lord is with you!"
2 Chronicles 20:17 NLT

God doesn't need you to help Him fight your battles. Just
stand still and take your position in Christ and watch Him
deliver you. Don't be afraid during the battle. Remember
His promises to you. If you allow fear to take over, you
will start making decisions that are not wise. Decisions that
are made from fear will cause more detriment than they
will help. He doesn't need you to struggle and strive and
reason this out to try to come up with a solution; just be
still and wait on Him. He is with you in this; if there is a
moment, He wants you to move, He will tell you. Until
then, rest, knowing that God loves you and He will give
you victory.

DAY 220

You Capture His Heart

You have captured my heart,
my treasure, my bride. You hold it hostage with one
glance of your eyes,
with a single jewel of your necklace.
Song of Songs 4:9 NLT

You have stolen God's heart. Every time He looks at you, His heart fills with pride to know that you are His. You are His beloved. God's love for you goes beyond the depths of anything you could imagine. When you worship, it steals His breath away. He loves to shine His light on you and through you so that everyone knows that you are His. God longs for the times when you come to Him and just sit and commune with Him. Like an earthly parent who cherishes their time with their kids, God cherishes His time with you. Every moment you have His full attention. God wants to give you the desires of your heart. You are safe with Him. You can tell Him all your secrets, even the ones you try to hide in the dark, and He will still love you. He will hold you and forgive you for all your sins. God will never reject you or condemn you. Trust your heart in His hands of love.

DAY 221

You Are Safe

Though I am surrounded by troubles, you will protect me from the anger of my enemies. You reach out your hand, and the power of your right hand saves me.
Psalm 138:7 NLT

God is an impenetrable fortress around you. He protects you from all our enemies. Like with Job, satan has no authority over your life and cannot come near you without God's permission. He will only allow what He knows is going to result in your good and His purpose. Everything is filtered through His hands of love for you. You can trust in His love. It is a firm foundation for you to stand on even when the storms rage all around you. God is always in control of every single detail. Satan is a defeated foe. He can scream loud, but ultimately, God has all authority. God is the one who controls how far the enemy can go. When it feels like you are surrounded, He will reach down and rescue you.

DAY 222

God Will Help

*So we can confidently say, "The Lord is my helper; I will
not fear; what can man do to me?"*
Hebrews 13:6 ESV

God is always here for you when you need Him. All you
must do is call His name. He wants to help you in every
situation you face. God doesn't want you to try to get
through this life alone and do things by the skin of your
teeth. He wants you to live a good life and enjoy life. Do
not go around worried about things all the time. Don't let
man's opinion or even his actions frighten you. God loves
you. He has forgiven you and washed away your shame.
God protects you, so there is nothing that you need to
worry about. Don't let life pass you by with frustration and
worry. Enjoy the little moments with your family. Enjoy
the gifts God has given you while you are here on this
earth, and remember this earth is not the end. There is more
to come after this.

DAY 223

God's Word Heals

He sent out his word and healed them, and delivered them from their destruction.
Psalm 107:20 ESV

God's Word, whether written or spoken, brings healing to every area of your life. When you are broken, He speaks peace over you. When you are sick, He speaks healing over you. When you are lonely and feel unloved, He speaks extravagant love over you. When you are lost in your sin, He speaks forgiveness over you. When you are bound in oppression, He speaks deliverance over you. Do not pay attention to any other voice. There is no one else who can speak and change things in your life. No one else's words carry life and healing in them. God's words are alive and active. They calm your fears and heal your soul. Rest in His words.

DAY 224

God's Arms Are Open

But you'll welcome us with open arms when we run for cover to you. Let the party last all night! Stand guard over our celebration. You are famous, God, for welcoming God-seekers, for decking us out in delight.
Psalm 5:11-12 MSG

God's arms are always open to you. No matter where you have been or what you have done, you can come boldly and confidently to Him. You never have to hang your head down in shame when you come to Him. He loves you, and He always has compassion for you. God loves it when you run to Him and ask Him for help. He wants you to have joy. He wants you to go through this journey of life with a smile on your face and laughter in your heart, not downtrodden and discouraged all the time. God loves to see the delight in your eyes. It brings Him joy to give you good gifts and rejoice in victories with you. He is not a fuddy-duddy God who wants you to be lowly and serious all the time. Enjoy life, have fun. Love your life! Jesus came to give you life more abundant; allow yourself to walk in that abundant life.

DAY 225

God's Family

So now you Gentiles are no longer strangers and foreigners. You are citizens along with all of God's holy people. You are members of God's family.
Ephesians 2:19 NLT

You are now part of God's very own family. You are no stranger to Him. He will never treat you as a stranger, but He will always welcome you in with open arms. You are His child. It gave Him so much pleasure to adopt you into His family through the blood of His Son. Nothing can separate you now, and no power in hell that can take you away from Him. He welcomes you in and gives you good gifts. You have His DNA running through your veins. You are no longer a citizen of this earth, but you are now a citizen of heaven, where you will rejoice and laugh and live together for eternity.

DAY 226

God Is Your Best Friend

The Lord is my shepherd;
I have all that I need.
Psalm 23:1 NLT

God knows there are times that you feel lonely. You feel like no one in the world sees you or cares about you. There are times you feel like you are the only one in the world going through the storms you are going through, and you just need someone to talk to. You are not alone! He is here. He sees you, and He knows you. Jesus has felt everything you feel. He understands your hurt and pain. He wants you to know that others are going through the things you are going through. Even when you have no one to talk to, you have Him. God is your very best friend! He will never reject you. You can share anything with Him, and He will not turn away from you. Because you have God, you have everything you need. He is more than enough!

DAY 227

God Cannot Lie

God is not a man, so he does not lie. He is not human, so he does not change his mind. Has he ever spoken and failed to act? Has he ever promised and not carried it through?
Numbers 23:19 NLT

God will never promise you something and not come through for you. He is not a man; He does not act the way that man acts. He is God! God cannot and will not ever lie. If He promises you something, He will never snatch it back from you or change His mind. That is not His character. God is kind and compassionate. He is faithful and trustworthy. God loves to fulfill His promises to you. Every single word that He has spoken will come to pass. Your mistakes and failures cannot stop His promises. Your fears for today or worries for tomorrow cannot stop His promises. No demon in hell or man on earth can stop His promises. Wait patiently for Him to act! He will do everything He said He would do.

DAY 228

Perfect Peace

You will keep in perfect peace all who trust in you, all whose thoughts are fixed on you!
Isaiah 26:3 NLT

When your thoughts are fixed on God, you will live this life in perfect peace. This world is chaotic and scary but remember that this world has no power over you because you are His, and He has overcome this world. You are in it now, but one day all of this will pass away. Do not fret when you see the wicked prospering; just keep your trust in God. When the great day comes that everyone stands before Him, prospering on this earth will not keep them from His judgment. Those who look to this world for their joy and peace will lose it quickly, but you will have joy for eternity because you trust in Him. God gives you peace that goes beyond anything this world will ever be able to understand. You have nothing to fear because He is with you always, even to the end of this world.

DAY 229

Fix Your Focus

*If you don't know, O most beautiful woman,
follow the trail of my flock, and graze your young goats
by the shepherds' tents.*
Song of Songs 1:8 NLT

God is always and will always be here for you. When you
start to lose focus and your world seems to be crashing in
around you, go to Him, cry out to Him. He will light your
way back to Himself. Bring Him all your cares and
burdens; you were not meant to carry them. Lay them
down at His feet and meet Him in the secret place where
His presence dwells. Sit with Him. Don't try to muster
anything up or say the right words; just sit with Him in the
quiet and let Him pour His love over you. You are His
heart's desire. You are His prized possession. He longs to
care for you and heal every broken part of you. Just come
before God honest and true, don't try to put on a mask. He
knows you anyway, even when you try to hide.

DAY 230

God's Love Is for Generations

*The wind blows, and we are gone—as though we had
never been here. But the love of the Lord remains forever
with those who fear him. His salvation extends to the
children's children*
Psalm 103:16-17 NLT

Life on earth is fleeting. You are here today, and then it
seems like life is over. After this is the best life, you could
imagine. You will be with God face-to-face every day.
You will see Him with your own eyes instead of Him
feeling invisible to you. Remember, though, that this life is
not the end. Even though this earth and life on it will pass
away, God's love for you will never pass away; it will
never change. His love will just pass from one life into the
other. It is not just for you, but for your children and your
children's children, through every generation.

DAY 231

Songs of Deliverance

*For you are my hiding place; you protect me from
trouble. You surround me with songs of victory.*
Psalm 32:7 NLT

God will cover you with His wings and protect you. He
tucks you away safely in His hiding place. He watches over
you carefully. He never takes His eyes off you. Like an
eagle watches over her nest, God watches over you. He
especially takes careful care of you when you are broken
and hurting. Like a mother whose child is sick, He pays
extra attention to you. He takes you in His arms and holds
you. He allows you to pour your heart out to Him without
judgment. He is okay when you feel your emotions and
process them with Him. It is okay to yell or to cry. Just
remember, this is not where you are staying; you are going
on to victory. He will put a new song in your heart. He
surrounds you with songs of deliverance.

DAY 232

Seek God Wholeheartedly

*I love those who love me, and those
who seek me diligently find me.*
Proverbs 8:17 ESV

When you seek God with all your heart, you will find Him.
When you make Him the one thing that is enough for you,
you will never lack what you need. He will take complete
and perfect care of you. It thrills His heart when you seek
Him above anything or anyone on the earth.

God loves to pour out His heart and His blessings on those
who love Him more than anything else. You will desire
Him more than the next breath you take when you realize
who He is and how much He loves you. God loves you
beyond the highest mountains, the deepest seas, or the
most expansive oceans. There is nothing that can measure
how big God's love is for you.

DAY 233

Just Be You

I have called you back from the ends of the earth,
saying, 'You are my servant.'
For I have chosen you
and will not throw you away.
Isaiah 41:9 NLT

Before the foundations of the earth, God chose you. He hand-picked you to be His. You are not only His child but His ambassador. You have been called to use your voice to tell of Jesus and His good news. God loves you! He has not rejected you and never will reject you. Even if everyone on the earth rejects you, He will always accept you and call you His. You have nothing to fear from God. You are completely safe with Him. He wants you to always be yourself in His presence and not try to be what you think He wants you to be. God wants you to be exactly like He created you to be because who He made you to be is marvelous to Him.

DAY 234

God Is Surrounding You

I lay down and slept;
I woke again, for the Lord sustained me.
I will not be afraid of many thousands of people
who have set themselves against me all around.
Psalm 3:5-6 ESV

When God is on your side, you are safe. You are surrounded by His presence every moment of the day. Even when it feels like the enemy is surrounding you, remember that He is with you, and you are hidden in the shadow of His wings. There is no demon in hell that can harm you when you put your trust in God. No matter what is going on all around you, you can be calm. You can lay your head down at night on your pillow and know that He is watching over you. His love quiets you and calms your mind. You never have anything to fear when God is on your side.

DAY 235

Sit With God

*My heart has heard you say, "Come and talk with me."
And my heart responds, "Lord, I am coming."*
Psalm 27:8 NLT

If you will quiet your mind and heart when there is so much noise and chaos swirling around you, if you lean in close, you will hear God's voice calling for you to come to be with Him. All He needs is your "Yes Lord." When you put aside everything else to be with Him, He will meet with you there, and He will speak to you. God will heal you when you meet Him in the secret place. If you allow Him into the places you have hidden away for so long, not allowing anyone into, He will bring restoration and wholeness to those places that have been broken. God is tender in His care. He will not rush you; He will carefully, slowly take you through the process of healing so that you will emerge with nothing missing and nothing lacking.

DAY 236

He Goes Before You & Behind You

*The priests will carry the Ark of the Lord, the Lord of all
the earth. As soon as their feet touch the water, the flow
of water will be cut off upstream,
and the river will stand up like a wall."*
Joshua 3:13 NLT

You do not have to have a fear of the future because God's presence goes before you in everything you do. He already knows what will happen before you get there, and He has a plan for every moment. There is nothing too big for Him to handle. God can move mountains if He needs to. He can open waters so you will walk through on dry ground. God is the God of Miracles, and wherever His presence is, a miracle can happen. Not only does He go before, but he also is behind you. Just like when the Israelites crossed the Red Sea, not only did He go before them and open the seas, but He was behind them and closed the waters, so their enemies drowned. He goes before, and He is behind you. God surround you on all sides, so every detail from every direction is taken care of so you can get to your promised land safely.

DAY 237

You Are Perfectly Crafted

And yet, O Lord, you are our Father.
We are the clay, and you are the potter.
We all are formed by your hand.
Isaiah 64:8 NLT

You are the marvelous work of God's hands. Like an artist sits at a potter's wheel and takes careful and intricate steps to make an exquisite piece of art, so it is with you. God was careful to knit every piece together perfectly in the image He wanted you to be when He created you. There is no other person on this earth like you. No one has your voice or your fingerprint. You are His masterpiece. Even the parts of you that you don't like, God loves. He made all of you. He wouldn't change a thing about you. When you look in the mirror every day, He wants you to remember that you were crafted by the Creator of the Universe. You were crafted carefully and intricately and perfectly by Him.

DAY 238

It's A Party

"Yes, God's Message: 'You're going to look at this place, these empty and desolate towns of Judah and streets of Jerusalem, and say, "A wasteland. Unlivable. Not even a dog could live here." But the time is coming when you're going to hear laughter and celebration, marriage festivities, people exclaiming, "Thank God-of-the-Angel-Armies. He's so good! His love never quits," as they bring thank offerings into God's Temple. I'll restore everything that was lost in this land. I'll make everything as good as new.' I, God, say so.
Jeremiah 33:10-11 MSG

When everything around you looks dead and desolate, when it seems like it is the end and there is no hope, that is when God will show up and blow your mind. It is when people look at something or someone and say there is no hope that God can show His power. He will take your mourning and turn it into dancing. He will take your tears and turn them into laughter. When He shows up, it will be time to throw a victory party! There will be singing and shouting instead of discouragement and dismay. He restores what looks like it is hopeless. He makes all things brand new. Never count anything out when you know God because He likes to do the impossible and take what is as dark as night and shine His light as bright as day!

DAY 239

God Hears Your Heart

*The Lord is near to the brokenhearted
and saves the crushed in spirit.*
Psalm 34:18 ESV

God is a God of compassion. He hurts when you hurt. It breaks His heart to see you cry. He is not a faraway God; He is close to you when you are broken. God draws you to Himself. He leans into your whispers when you can barely get out the words. Even when you have no words to say, He hear the cries of your heart. God grieves with you when you grieve. He is always here for you. He will hold you tight, close to His chest until you are ready to move. God will never rush you; He is patient and kind. He will give you the time you need to walk through the healing process when you have been crushed. Run to Him. He is here with open arms waiting to comfort you. He will turn your mourning to dancing and your sorrow to joy when you are ready.

DAY 240

God Is Here To The End

Teach these new disciples to obey all the commands I have given you. And be sure of this: I am with you always, even to the end of the age."
Matthew 28:20 NLT

God has promised He will never leave you or abandon you. He will never leave you to fend for yourself in this life. God will teach you His ways, and He will stay with you always. Until this earth has come to an end and the new heaven and new earth are here, He will not leave your side for one moment. God is with you, and He is in you. You have nothing to fear because you are never alone. No matter what you face, He will give you strength and grace to walk through it while He is walking beside you holding your hand, and when it gets too hard, and you feel weak, He will carry you until you can walk again. God loves you.

DAY 241

God Will Not Fail

For God alone, O my soul, wait in silence,
for my hope is from him.
He only is my rock and my salvation,
my fortress; I shall not be shaken.
Psalm 62:5-6 ESV

God knows there are times that you have been crying out to Him for a long time to rescue you from the circumstances you are in, and you don't understand why He hasn't. God needs you to know that He loves you so much, and He would never do anything to harm you in any way. He also needs you to trust Him, that He has your absolute best interest at heart. God sees beyond this moment into tomorrow. He sees things that you cannot see and knows things you cannot know, and He protects you.

Keep your gaze focused on Him, and remember that He is good, and He does good. His timing is perfect, and His promises always prove true. His presence wraps around you on all sides. Know that He is always working on your behalf, even when it doesn't look like it. Just trust Him as you wait! He will never fail you. If He has made you a promise, it will be carried out. Don't give up; take heart and wait for Him.

DAY 242

There Is Nothing He Won't Do

He who did not spare His own Son, but delivered Him up
for us all, how shall He not with Him also
freely give us all things?
Romans 8:32 NKJV

If God loves you so much that He gave up His one and only Son for you, do you really think there is anything He wouldn't do for you? Jesus was His prized possession. If He did not even hold Him back, why would you believe that He would keep healing from you or deliverance from you, or forgiveness from you? God does not dangle things in front of you and then snatch them away. If there is something you are asking for and He is not giving it to you, then you can trust that there is a reason that He knows that you cannot see why He is not answering that prayer. He will always do what is best for you. You can absolutely trust Him with everything in your life. There is nothing you cannot ask Him for.

DAY 243

God's Image

So the Word became human and made his home among
us. He was full of unfailing love and faithfulness. And we
have seen his glory, the glory of the Father's
one and only Son.
John 1:14 NLT

Jesus was born into this world as a man. He was the Son
of Man, yet also the Son of God. He was the Word made
flesh and dwelling right here on this earth. He came to die
for you. He was the very image of who God is. Just as He
was full of unfailing love, God is full of unfailing love. Just
as He was full of faithfulness, God is full of faithfulness.
Jesus walked the earth full of compassion and grace and
wanted you to see and understand that just as He was, so is
God. God is not the god that a lot of people thought He was
before Jesus came. When you look into the eyes of Jesus,
you are looking into God's eyes. God is kind, and He wants
you to know that He loves you, and you can trust Him with
everything in your life.

DAY 244

Dream Big

Delight yourself in the Lord, and he will give you the
desires of your heart.
Psalm 37:4 ESV

It thrills God's heart when you delight yourself in Him. He is always delighted with you.

You are the apple of God's eye! You steal His heart away. He loves to hear your voice lifted to Him, whether in prayer or worship. When your hearts are entwined together, He is beaming from ear to ear. When you take the time to let Him into your life and help you in every detail, from the good to the bad, He will begin to place His desires in your heart. Not only will He put His desires in your heart, but He will fulfill those desires. He wants you to dream together, to live this life together, to work together. He wants you to dream big and watch Him make those dreams come true. Sometimes you limit yourself, and you limit God when you dream too small. God loves to do big things for you because you are His child. Today allow yourself to dream the dreams you have been afraid to dream, knowing that no, you can't do those things, but God can!

DAY 245

Freely Receive

Because you are precious in my eyes,
and honored, and I love you,
I give men in return for you,
peoples in exchange for your life.
Isaiah 43:4 ESV

Do you even realize how precious and valuable you really are to God. He would do anything for you when He knows it is for your good. Not because you can earn it with your works, or because you can behave well enough for it. Not because you have pulled yourself up by your bootstraps and made something happen. Not because of your great intellect, but simply because He loves you and want to. He loves you so much that He gave Jesus in your place. There is no greater love than this. People may do something for you if you have done something for them or know they will get something in exchange, but God has done everything for you wanting nothing in return, except a relationship with you. He has freely given all He has for you. All you need to do is freely receive His love and affections for you. Just open your heart and receive.

DAY 246

Put Your Eyes On God

He lets me rest in green meadows; he leads me
beside peaceful streams.
Psalm 23:2 NLT

Amidst the turmoil, if you run to God, He will give you rest. He will lead you to green meadows to lie down and just breathe. God provides you with peace in the middle. When the winds and waves are blowing all around you, right in the middle, just like Jesus, you can lie down your head and sleep in the boat. God will lead you beside quiet waters where you will find life and be rejuvenated. Peaceful streams where you can sit and just listen to His voice and soak in His love for you.

Right smack dab in the middle of all the chaos and turmoil, you will be calm and quiet because of who you are and Whose you are. No one and nothing on the earth can do that for you. Just put your eyes on God.

DAY 247

God Planned Your Life Journey

O Lord, you are my God;
I will exalt you; I will praise your name,
for you have done wonderful things,
plans formed of old, faithful and sure.
Isaiah 25:1 ESV

Before He created the earth's foundations, before He flung the stars in the sky, God knew you and made plans for you. He smiled as He carefully thought through your journey on this earth.

It gave Him joy as He wrote down each moment that you and He would walk together. Planning the day you would take your first breath, the day you would smile for the first time. When you would take your first step. All the significant moments of your life He knew already before you even got there. Every moment of your story was carefully and intricately thought through in His heart of love for you. God saw the moments of pain and sorrow and the moments of joy and laughter. And every moment He planned; He will fulfill in your life. He loves watching each moment unfold and seeing your wonder and amazement at the work of His hands.

DAY 248

Mourning To Joy

*For his anger lasts only a moment, but his favor lasts a
lifetime! Weeping may last through the night, but joy
comes with the morning*
Psalm 30:5 NLT

God is slow to get angry and filled with unfailing love. His
anger is always towards His enemy, not toward you, His
child. God only ever loves you. He pours His favor out on
your life each day. The little things that happen that you
wonder why, like someone giving you something for
nothing, or you stand out above the rest, getting a good
deal when no one else did, that is God's favor being poured
out on you. With that favor comes His joy and unfailing
love. There will be days when you feel like you can't go
on, but just hold on because there will be joy when there is
mourning. God will turn the hard things into good things
in your life. It looks dark just before the sun rises. These
dark times are the times you must remind yourself that
things can change at any moment. Don't give up; just wait
for the sun; it will shine again!

DAY 249

Dive To The Depths

For your steadfast love is great to the heavens,
your faithfulness to the clouds.
Be exalted, O God, above the heavens!
Let your glory be over all the earth!
Psalm 57:10-11 ESV

God's love for you cannot even be fathomed! It is higher than the highest of highs; it reaches the lowest of lows. His love is the most powerful force in your life. It wraps around you and protects you. His faithfulness to you is a solid foundation for your feet. You can count on Him in all things. God cares about the tiniest details. He will always be faithful to you, even when you have doubts and unbelief. God's glory will show over all the earth. He is the Lord of lords and the King of kings. He is holy and righteous. God is beyond anything you will ever comprehend. You can dive to the depths of who He is and never reach the bottom. You will spend your life getting to know Him and unearthing new treasures every day. God is the one true God, and you are the focus of His thoughts and love.

DAY 250

Don't Hide From God

But you, O Lord, are a God merciful and gracious,
slow to anger and abounding in steadfast
love and faithfulness.
Psalm 86:15 ESV

As your Father, it is God's pleasure to take perfect and complete care of you. He is a gentle Father. He is a Father who loves to give you good gifts. God is protective of you. He is not waiting to punish you but to lavish His love on you. God's love never fails you; it never gives up on you. His love never abandons you. God loves to sit with you and have a conversation. He wants you to trust Him with everything in your life. God doesn't want you to hide anything from Him. He already knows you better than you know yourself. There is nothing you can tell Him that will surprise Him or make Him leave you. God's grace always picks you up and dusts you off, and helps you move forward. He is right here for you always.

DAY 251

Walk In Blessings

*But Christ has rescued us from the curse pronounced by
the law. When he was hung on the cross, he took upon
himself the curse for our wrongdoing. For it is written in
the Scriptures, "Cursed is everyone
who is hung on a tree."*
Galatians 3:13 NLT

Jesus came and died for you. He took the curse of sin for
you. Now instead of you being punished for your sin, you
are accepted and forgiven. You have been redeemed and
washed clean by His blood. He hung on the tree for you,
and He did it with joy because of God's great love for
you. You have been rescued from darkness and placed in
the Light. Now there is no more condemnation for you.
Instead of walking in the curse of the law, you now walk
in God's blessings because you believed in Jesus. This new
life you have, walking in His love and grace, no one can
take away from you. It was sealed with the blood of Jesus.

DAY 252

God Will Not Abandon You

No one will be able to stand against you as long as you live. For I will be with you as I was with Moses. I will not fail you or abandon you.
Joshua 1:5 NLT

You have nothing to fear in this life or in death. God is with you always. He will never leave your side or leave you without help. The enemy has no chance against you because you are God's. You can come to Him no matter what, and He will help you. God will never fail you. He will always give you wisdom for whatever you are facing if you will just ask. A lot of things in this life you don't have because you simply don't ask. God wants to help you. He wants to give you answers. Just ask Him. God will never abandon you; in good times and bad times, He will be right here with you. God wants you to involve Him in every detail of your life. He doesn't want you to just talk to Him when things are going bad, but He wants you to tell Him about the good stuff too.

DAY 253

Salvation Is A Gift

For by grace you have been saved through faith. And this is not your own doing; it is the gift of God, not a result of works, so that no one may boast.
Ephesians 2:8-9 ESV

Salvation is a gift that you cannot earn. Salvation can only be found in Jesus, and it is only given by faith. It is purely a gift that was paid for by the blood of Jesus. You cannot be good enough for it, and you cannot work enough for it. Because you didn't earn it, you cannot boast about it and think that you are better than anyone else. All you must do is believe it, and you receive it. It is so simple, yet so many miss it because they try to do something for it. Come to God as you are. You don't have to clean yourself up first. No one will be turned away from this gift. It is evidence of His great love for you.

DAY 254

Showers Of Blessing

*And I will make them and the places all around my hill a
blessing, and I will send down the showers in their
season; they shall be showers of blessing.*
Ezekiel 34:26 ESV

All things are in God's timing. His timing is perfect. Just
when it looks like everything is going to be over, God will
show up. He will send His rain right on time. Just like it
rained manna from heaven for the Israelites, He will give
you exactly what you need at the exact right time. Be
patient while you wait, knowing that His ways are perfect,
and all His promises are true. Hold tight to your faith, and
you will see God rain down showers of blessings that you
cannot begin to contain. God will bless everything you put
your hands to. He will bless your children and their
children. He will pour out His blessings without fail on
those who hold on and wait patiently for Him to act.

DAY 255

Cry Out To God

But in my distress I cried out to the Lord; yes, I prayed to my God for help. He heard me from his sanctuary; my cry to him reached his ears.
Psalm 18:6 NLT

When you cry out to God for help, He will always hear your cry. He hears you from His secret place, and He will always help you. Keep your eyes open for God's help because it may not always come in the way you think it will, but it will always come. It may not come when you want it to, but it will always come. While you wait for the answer, keep your eyes fixed on Him, and He will give you His peace. God will never leave you alone to have to come up with your own solutions. God will always give you the wisdom to either stand still or move. Just be obedient to His voice and leave the results to Him.

DAY 256

Release It All To God

Cast your burden on the Lord [releasing the weight of it]
and He will sustain you; He will never allow the
[consistently] righteous to be moved
(made to slip, fall, or fail).
Psalm 55:22 AMPC

You were not meant to carry your burdens on your shoulders. You will crumble under the weight of them. God wants you to bring all your burdens to Him. He wants you to cast them on Him. God can handle them better than you ever could. He knows exactly how to care for you in every situation. Those family members you are worried about and praying for, God loves them even more than you do. He will take care of them. God doesn't want you to just lay it down for a little while and pick it back up; He wants you to release it to Him completely and leave it there. If you do this, He will sustain you. He will give you His peace while you wait for Him to come through for you. You can enjoy life while you wait. Your joy is not based on your circumstances but on the fact that He is with you and will take care of you no matter what is going on around you. God will never fail you or loosen His grip on you.

DAY 257

God Will Blow Your Mind

That is what the Scriptures mean when they say, "No eye has seen, no ear has heard, and no mind has imagined what God has prepared for those who love him."
1 Corinthians 2:9 NLT

There are so many things God wants to unfold in your life and blow your mind with. You cannot even begin to imagine all the good things He has for your life because you love Him. Not only in this life but also for eternity to come. God will take care of you because you trust Him and know Him as your God. His ways go far beyond anything you could dream up in your wildest dreams. God loves to pour His blessings out on those who are faithful to Him. He can do anything, and He has all the resources He needs to do it. God is so excited about the things He planned for you. God cannot wait to see your face when He brings them to fruition in your life! Get ready; when God shows up, all will know that you are His child.

DAY 258

Sometimes The Answer Is A Whisper

"He stood before me and said, 'Daniel, I have come to make things plain to you. You had no sooner started your prayer when the answer was given. And now I'm here to deliver the answer to you. You are much loved! So listen carefully to the answer, the plain meaning of what is revealed:
Daniel 9:22-23 MSG

As soon as you pray to God, He hears you and answers you. Sometimes the answer doesn't get to you exactly when you want it to, but you must trust God's timing. Sometimes the answer doesn't look like you want it to, but you must trust His ways. Everything He does is perfect for you. He knows you inside and out. He will not ever give you something that you are not ready for. God will not give you something that is going to do more harm to you than good. He loves you so much, and He will protect you and tenderly care for you. God will always answer you just listen carefully because sometimes you are waiting for a roar and the answer comes in a whisper.

DAY 259

All Your Life God Is There

The Lord rescues the godly; he is their fortress in times of trouble. The Lord helps them, rescuing them from the wicked. He saves them, and they find shelter in him.
Psalm 37:39-40 NLT

God is your Strong Tower. You can run to Him, and you are safe. God is your Impenetrable Fortress. When you trust in Him, the enemy cannot touch you. He is your Ever-present Help in trouble. He will rescue you from any pit you fall into. God is your Shelter. You can find cover in Him during any storm. God is all you will ever need. He is more than enough for you. When you find yourself at the end of all you know to do, and you don't think you can make it another day, God will see you through. He will carry you when you are too weak to walk. He will defend you when accused unjustly. God is the One who loves you and cares for you your whole life through.

DAY 260

God Covers You

But let all who take refuge in you rejoice;
let them sing joyful praises forever.
Spread your protection over them,
that all who love your name may be filled with joy.
For you bless the godly, O Lord;
you surround them with your shield of love.
Psalm 5:11-12 NLT

When you make God your hiding place, He will cover you and protect you in everything. You can trust Him with your very life. He is the One who makes every heartbeat and gives you every breath. When you put yourself on God's side, you will never regret it. Your days will be filled with joy and singing. Even amidst sorrow, you can rejoice when you make Him your Lord. He will wrap Himself around you and give you His peace. You will live under the shelter of His love and grace. God will defend you and heal you. He will pour out His blessings over your life and generations to come. You will leave a legacy for those who come after you of His power and goodness.

DAY 261

Your Past Is Gone

"I—yes, I alone—will blot out your sins for my own sake and will never think of them again.
Isaiah 43:25 NLT

God is the only one who can forgive your sins. If you turn to Him and walk away from your sin, He will make you as white as snow. This happens through the blood of Jesus. God did this so that you and He could have a relationship together, so that sin would no longer be able to separate you. Once you come to God for forgiveness, He will throw your sin as far as the east is from the west and never, ever remember it again. He will never bring it up and remind you of your past.

God wants you to forget the things behind you and look forward to the things that are ahead. Run your race with confidence that you are cleansed from all your wrongdoing, and you are extravagantly loved by Him. God keeps no record of wrongs. The enemy will try to bring up your past, but you just remind him that you were purchased with the blood of Jesus, which was his demise.

DAY 262

Enjoy This Moment

"Give your entire attention to what God is doing right now, and don't get worked up about what may or may not happen tomorrow. God will help you deal with whatever hard things come up when the time comes.
Matthew 6:34 MSG

Be present in everything you do. Enjoy the moment you are in, don't think about what was or what will be. Don't worry about what might happen in the future or how to take care of yourself or your family. Just keep your eyes focused on God, and He will get you safely to where you need to be in every situation. He prepares you all along the way for the next step you will take in front of you so that you will be ready when you get to that thing you have been worrying about. If you spend all your time worrying about what will happen next, you will use all the strength you will need when you get there on the worry. You will miss so many precious moments in life looking behind or ahead of you. Focus on now. You can't change anything with your worry. It will only serve to hurt you, not help you. Trust that God will take care of you and keep you safe and that He will give you His favor in every situation. Enjoy this moment!

DAY 263

Take Heart

"Don't let your hearts be troubled. Trust in God, and
trust also in me.
John 14:1 NLT

Do not be afraid. You have nothing to fear, God is your
God, and He is with you. He knows it is hard sometimes
not to let the fear take over. This world you live in is a
scary place. He doesn't condemn you or get mad at you
when you feel fear. He just wants you to get to the point
that His love for you always drives out the fear. God loves
you so much, and His promise to you is that He will take
care of you.

The fear is such a liar, and it wants you to lose sight of God
and think that you must be in control and keep yourself
safe, but that control and safety are an illusion. God is the
only one who is in control. Take heart and don't be
troubled by this world. Please just trust Him. Trust in the
blood that Jesus shed for you at the cross. That blood
stripped death of its power and defeated every foe. God is
here for you. Let Him have all your fears.

DAY 264

Process Your Healing With God

I will heal their waywardness. I will love them lavishly.
My anger is played out.
Hosea 14:4 MSG

You can come to God even when you have fallen. He will help you get back up and walk again. He will wash away your shame and sin and forget it for good. God will heal every broken part of you that runs to find things to satisfy you. Sometimes when you fall, you allow the guilt to take over, and you hide from Him, but He does not want this for you; He wants you to run to Him and let Him process through the healing with you. There are reasons that you run to your sin and addictions. There are broken places within you that you are trying to fill, but God is the only one who can fill those places in you. He is not angry with you. He will never be angry with you. God loves you so much, and He always will. You are the apple of His eye.

DAY 265

The Spirit Prays For You

*And the Holy Spirit helps us in our weakness. For
example, we don't know what God wants us to pray for.
But the Holy Spirit prays for us with groanings that
cannot be expressed in words. And the Father who
knows all hearts knows what the Spirit is saying, for the
Spirit pleads for us believers in harmony
with God's own will.*
Romans 8:26-27 NLT

There are times when you just do not have the words to
pray. Sometimes it just hurts too bad to try to find the
words. Other times you are just physically, emotionally, or
spiritually exhausted, and your mind needs a break. No
matter what the situation, when you find yourself unable
to pray, don't feel guilty or defeated because one of the
functions of the Holy Spirit is to pray for you. When you
don't have the words, the Holy Spirit will intercede on
your behalf, and God knows what the Spirit is saying even
when you don't. Everything that the Spirit prays for you
will always align with God's will for your life. So, when
you don't have the words, just let the Spirit speak for you.
It may just be in a cry, a groan, a laugh, but it will be
precisely what the Father wants.

DAY 266

No Need To Fear

*Don't be afraid, for I am with you. Don't be discouraged,
for I am your God. I will strengthen you and help you. I
will hold you up with my victorious right hand*
Isaiah 41:10 NLT

Do not let fear paralyze your life. You never have to be
afraid because God is with you in everything. Not only is
He with you, but He is inside you. The same Spirit that
raised Christ from the dead lives and moves in you. You
never have to live in discouragement because He is your
God. He is the One who created everything out of nothing,
and He is the One who loves you extravagantly and has
adopted you as His child. Nothing is impossible for Him.
He is the Great I Am! Your life is safe with God. He will
hold you tight and never let you go. God holds you with
His victorious right hand. If you stay with Him and trust
His ways, you will walk in victory and see your promised
land. Fear is a liar!

DAY 267

Praise God At All Times

I will praise You, O Lord, with my whole heart; I will show forth (recount and tell aloud) all Your marvelous works and wonderful deeds!

I will rejoice in You and be in high spirits; I will sing praise to Your name, O Most High!
Psalm 9:1-2 AMPC

Your praise is a sweet-smelling fragrance to God. It is a sweet sound to His ears. When you lift your praise in the middle of your storm, it causes the enemy to be confused. Praise God even before you see your breakthrough. Remember when Paul and Silas lifted their praises to God in prison, the chains broke, and prison doors were opened. He is so honored by your praise. At your praise, mountains crumble, and demons flee. When your thoughts are chaotic, and you can't stop the swirling and the noise, stop, and lift His name in praise, and you will see them begin to calm because you switched your focus to God instead of your worries. Praise God when it is good and praise God when it is bad. Always lift your praise.

DAY 268

Love Like This

*We know what real love is because Jesus gave up his life
for us. So we also ought to give up our lives for our
brothers and sisters.*
1 John 3:16 NLT

Jesus was an example to you of real love. He laid down His
life for you even when you were still a sinner. He poured
out His love for you at a cross. God's hope is that you too
will show this kind of love to those around you. Love
unconditionally. Love in the good and in the bad. Love
without expecting anything back from anyone. Love
because God loved you first. He has loved you
extravagantly and forgiven all your sins. Forgive quickly,
as He does. Love extravagantly. Feed the hungry, help the
poor, rescue the oppressed. When you do these things, you
are showing that you are His child. The more you pour out
the love He gives you, the more you realize what love
really looks like. You must let God love you first or you
will have nothing to pour out. You never have to worry that
you will not be loved because He will always pour His love
into you so that you will be full too.

DAY 269

Body, Soul, & Spirit

*May God himself, the God who makes everything holy
and whole, make you holy and whole, put you together—
spirit, soul, and body—and keep you fit for the coming of
our Master, Jesus Christ. The One who called you is
completely dependable. If he said it, he'll do it!*
1 Thessalonians 5:23-24 MSG

God will do a complete work in you. What He has started,
He will finish. He will not leave any part of you untouched.
When He does a complete healing, it is not just healing
your body, but it is your body, your soul, and your spirit.
God goes to the broken places that you try to hide from
everyone else, and He draws them out into the light gently
and tenderly and takes you through the process of healing
with Him. God is trustworthy. He will never fail you. He
cannot fail. Just as He cannot fail, He cannot lie. If He has
given you a promise, it will absolutely happen. It may not
happen like you think it should or how you hoped it would.
It may not happen when you think it should, but it will
happen, and the way and timing of it all will be perfect.
God will complete you and keep you until the day you live
with Him forever.

DAY 270

Never-ending Joy

*Those who have been ransomed by the Lord will
return. They will enter Jerusalem singing,
crowned with everlasting joy.
Sorrow and mourning will disappear,
and they will be filled with joy and gladness.*
Isaiah 51:11 NLT

Joy is a healing balm for your whole being. When you are joyful, you have laughter. Laughter is good medicine. When you are joyful, you look forward to the days ahead. You look to the future with hope, excitement, and expectation of good. When you have the joy that God gives you, no one can take it away from you. It isn't based on your circumstances changing, but it is based on who you are and knowing who your Father is. Depression and discouragement cannot abide where God's joy is; it will drive them out. Joy causes you to sing a new song of praise. It will cause you to dance when no music is playing. It is like a fountain bubbling up in your soul. You can have joy because God will come through for you. He will set you free and put your feet on solid ground. He will never abandon you. He is your portion, and He will always love you!

DAY 271

Wonders Of God's Love

Praise the Lord, for he has shown me the wonders of his unfailing love. He kept me safe when my city was under attack. In panic I cried out, "I am cut off from the Lord!" But you heard my cry for mercy and answered my call for help.
Psalm 31:21-22 NLT

The moment you cry out to God in distress, He will answer you. His ears are always attentive to the sound of your voice. He will rescue you and deliver you from the darkness. His light invades the darkness, and the darkness cannot put it out. God will keep you safe and protect you in everything. You are never alone. God is not a distant Father, but He is right there with you in every single moment. Because God loves you, He will answer you. He will show His power to all your enemies. They will not conquer you. You are never fighting for victory; you are always fighting from victory because of the finished work of Jesus on the cross. God is your Hiding Place, your Strong Tower. He is the One who defends you in everything.

DAY 272

Follow God Not Man

O our God, will you not execute judgment on them? For we are powerless against this great horde that is coming against us. We do not know what to do, but our eyes are on you."
2 Chronicles 20:12 ESV

When it feels like you are surrounded, and you cannot find your way out, call on God, and He will give you wisdom. When you seek Him in every situation, He will show you the way out. He will come to your rescue when you are powerless to defeat your enemies. God will never leave you to fend for yourself. If you will, just trust Him and call on Him. Call on God instead of running to a man. He is the only one who has all wisdom and all power. Man's ideas and reasoning cannot save you from your enemies. Man will fail you, but God will never fail you. Come to Him, ask Him, and then do what He leads you to do, no matter what man tells you. Even if someone you think is very spiritual gives you instructions, and you know it isn't what God is saying, you must follow God. Everyone around you will see His power in your life when you choose to acknowledge Him and His wisdom instead of man.

DAY 273

Grace After Grace

*Change your life, not just your clothes. Come back to
God, your God. And here's why: God is kind and
merciful. He takes a deep breath, puts up with a lot, This
most patient God, extravagant in love, always ready to
cancel catastrophe. Who knows? Maybe he'll do it now,
maybe he'll turn around and show pity. Maybe, when
all's said and done, there'll be blessings full
and robust for your God!*
Joel 2:13-14 MSG

God is patient and kind. His unfailing love reaches to a
thousand generations. God does not pour out anger and
punishment upon you, but He pours out love and mercy.
Every time you run to Him for forgiveness, you will
receive it. God will never hold a grudge or remember your
past. He will draw you to Himself and give you hope for
the future. He washes away all your guilt and shame. When
you run to God, He takes your cheeks in His hands, and He
tells you how proud He is of you, how pleased He is with
you, and how much He loves you. God gives you grace
after grace after grace. He will never answer you with a
harsh answer or turn His face from you when you seek
Him. God is out for your good and showers you with His
love like standing under Niagara Falls.

DAY 274

You Are His Priority

The Lord protects those of childlike faith;
I was facing death, and he saved me.
Let my soul be at rest again,
for the Lord has been good to me.
Psalm 116:6-7 NLT

God wants you to learn to relax and rest in His presence. Don't be in a hurry all the time. He wants you to know that He is always protecting you. God will always be here for you. When you are broken and vulnerable, He will hide you away in His secret place until you are strong again. All He asks of you is that you trust Him. Trust Him with your whole heart and lay everything at His feet. He wants to take care of you. He wants you to know how precious you are to Him. God would never allow the enemy to harm you. He will always run to your rescue, even in times that you get yourself into trouble. Lean into Him, rely on Him. Let God be your best friend. He loves to be with you in everything. You are His priority.

DAY 275

You Know The Truth

We know that none of the God-born makes a practice of sin—fatal sin. The God-born are also the God-protected. The Evil One can't lay a hand on them. We know that we are held firm by God; it's only the people of the world who continue in the grip of the Evil One. And we know that the Son of God came so we could recognize and understand the truth of God—what a gift!—and we are living in the Truth itself, in God's Son, Jesus Christ. This Jesus is both True God and Real Life. Dear children, be on guard against all clever facsimiles.
1 John 5:18-21 MSG

You are God's child, and He loves you so much. He has you safe in His hands, and the enemy cannot touch you. God has a firm grip on you, and He will not loosen it. Those who do not know Him as their Father do not understand the truth, and they are still in the grips of the devil. Be on alert for this enemy of yours. He will try to tell you that God cannot protect you and that God will fail you, but hold on to the truth, which is Jesus. Hold onto the truth that God will never fail you or abandon you. The devil is a liar and the father of lies, and there is absolutely no truth to anything he says. Be on guard against the people of this world who the enemy uses to try to pull you and distract you away from God. Keep your eyes and your thoughts on God.

DAY 276

Breathe & Lean Into God

As a father shows compassion to his children,
so the Lord shows compassion to those who fear him.
For he knows our frame,
he remembers that we are dust.
Psalm 103:13-14 ESV

The love of a father on the earth cannot begin to compare with the love God has for you. Even if your earthly father would walk away from you or break a promise, God never will.

God is enthralled with you. He knows you from the inside out; you do not have to try to hide anything from Him. He already knows everything about you, and He still loves you. God understands that you are hurt sometimes. He knows you fail and make mistakes. It is okay. He will always be here for you. God's love is unconditional and unwavering toward you. You can trust Him with everything concerning your heart. He tenderly holds you in His hands. He will never be harsh with you. Just breathe and lean into Him. Everything will be okay.

DAY 277

Live By Faith In Jesus

I have been crucified with Christ. It is no longer I who live, but Christ who lives in me. And the life I now live in the flesh I live by faith in the Son of God, who loved me and gave himself for me.
Galatians 2:20 ESV

You are not alone in this world, and you do not have to do life all alone. Not only is Jesus, with you, but His Spirit lives in you. Everything you do and everywhere you go, He is with you. You can trust your life with Him. If He loved you so much that He died for you, there isn't one thing He wouldn't help you with or do for you. Remember that the Greater One lives and moves in you when life seems to knock you down, and you have no strength left. He brings life to you both here and into eternity. Put your whole faith into Him, and you will be able to rest and have peace no matter what happens in this world. He is with you. He is in you. You have absolutely nothing to fear!

DAY 278

You Will Be A Lighthouse

For great is your steadfast love toward me;
you have delivered my soul from the depths of Sheol.
Psalm 86:13 ESV

When you walk through what seems like the darkest time of your life, and there appears to be no way out, and you cannot see a glimmer of light, God will be there. He will rescue you from the deepest, darkest pit. Even when death is at your doorstep, He can deliver you and set you in a bright and spacious place. God loves you with everything within Him, and He is always looking out for your good. When He delivers you, He will shine His glory through you so that others can find hope and deliverance in their lives. If He can do it for you, He can do it for them. Let your voice be heard of how God came through for you when you get to the other side of this place. You will be a lighthouse directing others to Him.

DAY 279

His Beautiful Child

You are beautiful, my darling, beautiful beyond words.
Your eyes are like doves
behind your veil. Your hair falls in waves,
like a flock of goats winding down the slopes of Gilead.
Song of Songs 4:1 NLT

You thrill God. You are beautiful to Him. God loves to see your face and hear your voice. He is so pleased with you. He delights in your devotion to Him. He sees your heart that seeks after Him with everything you have. God sees you pouring out your life and your love to those around you for His glory. Because of your devotion to Him, He will honor you. He will shine the light of His glory and grace upon your life. You will consistently walk in His favor and His love.

It makes God so happy to live this life with you each day. He will bless you beyond your imaginations because you make Him your One thing.

DAY 280

Watch For God's Goodness

How kind the Lord is! How good he is!
So merciful, this God of ours!
Psalm 116:5 NLT

God loves to pour His kindness out on you. It is His pleasure to plan and do good things for His children. God loves it when you run to Him with boldness and confidence to receive His mercy. God never want you to cower in fear in His presence. He has no intentions of harm to you at any time, no matter what you have done. It thrills Him to be good to you and bless you in front of a world that is watching. They will see how good your Father is and want to taste for themselves and know that He is good. You make Him smile. Go out today and watch all around you and hide in your heart all the times you recognize His hand of goodness and love in your life.

DAY 281

Act Like It's Already Done

Though the cherry trees don't blossom and the strawberries don't ripen, Though the apples are worm-eaten and the wheat fields stunted, Though the sheep pens are sheepless and the cattle barns empty, I'm singing joyful praise to God. I'm turning cartwheels of joy to my Savior God. Counting on God's Rule to prevail, I take heart and gain strength. I run like a deer. I feel like I'm king of the mountain!
Habakkuk 3:17-19 MSG

Even when there are no signs of anything changing, even when you see no evidence of growth or God's hand at work, you can be sure things are happening. Before you even see the evidence and have tangible proof, let praises come from your lips because you can be sure that He is faithful and trustworthy, and when He gives you a promise, you can take it to the bank. Rejoice now as if it is already complete! When you do this, it will strengthen your spirit. It will give you joy and peace in the waiting! It will even strengthen your physical body when you are joyful and expectant. Don't put a timeline on it; just enjoy the waiting. Act as if you already have it in your hands and know that your promise is on the way!

DAY 282

There Is Power In Jesus Name

The name of the Lord is a strong fortress;
the godly run to him and are safe.
Proverbs 18:10 NLT

Jesus' name is greater than any other name. There is no other name that can set demons to flight. There is no other name that can heal the sick. There is no other name that can save a soul. His name is a strong and mighty hiding place for you. When you are struggling and feel like you can't go on, if all you can get out of your mouth is Jesus, then that is enough. There is wondering working power in Jesus' name. When you run to Him, you are safe. Nothing can stand against His name. Every knee will one day bow, and every tongue will confess that Jesus Christ is Lord. Just say His name; that is all you need.

DAY 283

Hide In The Secret Place

Because you have made the Lord your refuge, and the
Most High your dwelling place, There shall no evil befall
you, nor any plague or calamity come near your
tent. For He will give His angels [especial] charge over
you To accompany and defend and preserve you in all
your ways [of obedience and service]. They shall bear
you up on their hands, lest you dash
your foot against a stone.
Psalm 91:9-12 AMPC

When you make God your dwelling place, He will hide
you in His sanctuary. He will keep you from harm. The
evil one will not be able to touch you when you make God
the One you trust more than anything or anyone. No
weapon formed against you will prosper. No evil will come
near you. No plague will invade your home. You will not
have to fear what the world fears. His angels are constantly
on guard around you to rescue you and protect you from
all the schemes of your enemy. When you are in trouble,
God will be there. He will deliver you and honor you and
keep your feet from stumbling. Abide in His secret place.
Hide under the shadow of His wings; you are safe there.

DAY 284

God Has Given You A Voice

God reached out, touched my mouth, and said, "Look!
I've just put my words in your mouth—hand-delivered!
See what I've done? I've given you a job to do among
nations and governments—a red-letter day! Your job is to
pull up and tear down, take apart and demolish,
And then start over, building and planting."
Jeremiah 1:9-10 MSG

God will use your voice for His Kingdom if you let Him.
You will never need to worry about what to say. He will
give you the right words at the right times. Don't try to
rehearse it in your head. He has a purpose for you. He has
chosen you to go and be a testimony of His goodness and
love. God wants you to rescue those who are oppressed.
Stand up for the weak and poor. Take care of the widows
and the orphans. He has given you authority over all the
enemy's schemes. You will tear down his plans using Jesus
name. You will demolish the strongholds that have been
built, and you will build new and lasting foundations based
on His love and grace. You do not have to be afraid
because it will never be you working in your own strength
to build His Kingdom, but God will always be the One
working in you and through you.

DAY 285

God's Got This

But he said to me, "My grace is sufficient for you, for my power is made perfect in weakness." Therefore I will boast all the more gladly of my weaknesses, so that the power of Christ may rest upon me.
2 Corinthians 12:9 ESV

When you walk in God's grace, no matter what is going on in your life, you will be okay. When you feel weak, that is when His power kicks in. The things you cannot do on your own, He will empower you to do. When you have prayed and prayed and asked God to do something for you, and you don't see the answer, rest in His grace. Whatever the circumstances, or situation you are facing, God will help you through. So, you can boast in weakness because you know that when you are weak, that is when God gets to come in and be strong and do things that go way beyond your imagination. When you feel like you cannot go another day, don't worry, Christ's power will rest on you and carry you through. Do not fear, God's got this!

DAY 286

The Final Say

Nothing, not even a mighty mountain, will stand in Zerubbabel's way; it will become a level plain before him! And when Zerubbabel sets the final stone of the Temple in place, the people will shout: 'May God bless it! May God bless it!
Zechariah 4:7 NLT

Nothing can stand in the way of you fulfilling your dreams and destiny when God is on your side. Every mountain in front of you will be leveled to the ground. When you are pursuing His dreams for you and fulfilling His call on your life, He will protect you, He will be with you and in you. There is no demon in hell that can stop what God has planned for you. Your doubts and fears cannot stop it. You may make your plans, but it is His plans for you that will prevail. When people watch the tapestry that He weaves through your life and bring you to the place of completion, it will be a mighty sign of who He is. God always has the final say in everything concerning you.

DAY 287

Hope Of A New Day

You have turned my mourning into joyful dancing. You have taken away my clothes of mourning and clothed me with joy, that I might sing praises to you and not be silent. O Lord my God, I will give you thanks forever!
Psalm 30:11-12 NLT

When you make God your Father, it is not over until He says it is over. He always has the final word in the lives of His children. Those who are still under the devil's control do not have the hope that you have. When all you see around you is night, you know that soon there will be light. When all you see is sorrow and mourning, you know that soon there will be joy and laughter. You will dance and rejoice again. You will sing His praises at the top of your lungs, and those still under the enemy's control will see, and they will want what you have. You will be able to tell them that it is God who gives you this joy and laughter and hope of a new day.

DAY 288

One & Only God

"But you are my witnesses, O Israel!" says the Lord.
"You are my servant.
You have been chosen to know me, believe in me,
and understand that I alone am God.
There is no other God— there never has been, and there
never will be. I, yes I, am the Lord,
and there is no other Savior.
Isaiah 43:10-11 NLT

God is constantly wooing you into His presence. He loves to be with you. He wants to continually show you more and more aspects of who He is. God knew you before you were ever placed in your mother's womb. He knew you intimately; now He wants you to know Him intimately. God wants you to feel safe with Him. God hopes you will trust in Him completely and know that there is no other god but Him. There is no other god who is personally involved as He is.

No other god who is a father and loves intimately as God does. God is the one and only true God. He is the only one who created everything out of nothing. He is the One who was and is and is to come. There is no one else like God.

DAY 289

Just Be Still

"Be still, and know that I am God! I will be honored by every nation. I will be honored throughout the world." The Lord of Heaven's Armies is here among us; the God of Israel is our fortress.
Psalm 46:10-11 NLT

God does not want you to try to figure everything out on your own. He wants you to just trust Him. Rest in Him. Be still and know that He is God, not you. Be still. Stop struggling and striving to be good enough to save yourself. Be still and watch Him do what He does best. Let Him be in control. Sit back and relax as He takes care of everything that concerns you. As you allow God to be God and you stop striving, He will do what He does best, miracles, and all will see that He is God, and His name will be honored throughout all the earth! All will know that He is alive, and He lives and breathes among them. They will see that they can put their trust in God, and He will be their fortress.

DAY 290

God Loves To Be Good

*Therefore the Lord waits to be gracious to you, and
therefore he exalts himself to show mercy to you. For the
Lord is a God of justice; blessed are all those
who wait for him.*
Isaiah 30:18 ESV

You are God's prized possession, and He loves to be good
to you. He loves to give to you freely and graciously all
that you need. God shows mercy when no one else does.
He is a kind and loving Father. He does not rejoice in
troubles or sorrows, but He loves to see you succeed. God
cares for those who have been hurt by injustice. God
watches out for the poor and the orphans. You will never
be sorry that you have put your trust in Him. You will
never be sorry when you wait patiently for Him, and do not
try to defend yourself or take things into your own hands.
When Abraham and Sarah tried to do things their own way
and bring their promise about, they learned that doing that
did not bring God's best for them. They then had a
situation they did not want to have to deal with. Wait on
God. He knows what is best, and He knows the best
timing. He will never fail you!

DAY 291

He Calms Your Thoughts

When doubts filled my mind,
your comfort gave me renewed hope and cheer.
Psalm 94:19 NLT

In those times when your mind is swirling and chaotic, run to God. Hide away in the secret place with Him. Tell Him all your worries and anxieties, and His presence will wrap around you and calm your thoughts. When you step into the atmosphere of His love, your fears have no chance. Just a few minutes with Him is all it takes to turn your thoughts around and walk away joyful rather than worried. His presence is like a cool drink of water to you. It is refreshing and brings life. Just breathe in and allow His love to wash over you. Being with you is the delight of His day!

DAY 292

Release Everything To God

*He said, "Listen, all you people of Judah and Jerusalem!
Listen, King Jehoshaphat! This is what the Lord says: Do
not be afraid! Don't be discouraged by this mighty army,
for the battle is not yours, but God's.*
2 Chronicles 20:15 NLT

You are wearing yourself out and getting frustrated
because you are trying to fight your battles independently.
God never asked you to take care of yourself. He invites
you to let Him take care of you. All you need to do is trust
Him, stand still, and let Him be your defender. When the
enemy comes after you, God will stand between you and
the enemy, hiding you behind Him. The devil has no
chance when God is fighting for you. You cannot win any
battles on your own. You will just stay exhausted all the
time. Take your hands off it. Release everything to God,
and He will take care of every detail. Rest, you are His
child. Just remind yourself who your Father is and rest.

DAY 293

You Are His

But now, O Jacob, listen to the Lord who created you. O Israel, the one who formed you says, "Do not be afraid, for I have ransomed you. I have called you by name; you are mine. When you go through deep waters, I will be with you. When you go through rivers of difficulty, you will not drown. When you walk through the fire of oppression, you will not be burned up; the flames will not consume you.
Isaiah 43:1-2 NLT

God is the One who has chosen you; you did not choose Him. He has redeemed you and purchased you with the price of the blood of Jesus. You have no reason to be afraid. If He would do this for you, there is nothing He wouldn't do. The enemy has no rights to you because you are His. When you feel like you are drowning and can't get out, He will rescue you. When you feel like you are walking through the fire like Shadrach, Meshach, and Abednego, He will be in the fire with you. It will not consume you. You will walk out unharmed and unbound, not even smelling a little bit like smoke. This is your confidence because you belong to God. He has called you by your name, and He loves you with all His heart.

DAY 294

God Is Faithful & Trustworthy

God's way is perfect.
All the Lord's promises prove true.
He is a shield for all who look to him for protection.
Psalm 18:30 NLT

When God acts on your behalf, you never have to wonder if what He has done is the right thing for you. You can always know that His ways are perfect. Remember, He sees things differently than you, and He knows things that you do not know. God's timing is perfect. He will never be too early or too late. Every single promise He has spoken to you will come to pass. He will never lie to you. He will never promise you something and not act. He will always come through. God is faithful to you. Not only will He always do what He says He will do, but He will also always protect you. He will be a shelter surrounding you on all sides. Release your life into His hands and trust Him and rest.

DAY 295

Wait On Him

But they who wait for the Lord shall renew their strength;
they shall mount up with wings like eagles; they shall run
and not be weary; they shall walk and not faint.
Isaiah 40:31 ESV

Wait on God. You will never regret waiting. When you wait on Him, instead of taking things into your own hands, you will be rewarded. You will soar over your storms instead of trying to fight through them. You will not grow weak and tired from fighting your own battles and being in control of everything. You will be able to walk and not grow weary. You will have all the strength you will need when your promise arrives if you wait on God because you haven't used all your strength to take care of yourself. Trusting in Him causes you to rest while you wait. Just like an eagle doesn't spend all its energy flapping its wings through a storm, it just allows the wind to carry it, so it will be with you when you wait on God, you will just spread your wings, and He will carry you through.

DAY 296

Tapestry Of Beauty

Yes, you have been with me from birth;
from my mother's womb you have cared for me.
No wonder I am always praising you!
My life is an example to many,
because you have been my strength and protection.
Psalm 71:6-7 NLT

From the day you were born into this world, God was taking care of you. He has already chosen you to be His. God was already completely in love with you. When you first spoke God's name, it thrilled His heart. When your little eyes opened, He saw you, and He knew you. God smiled. You are such an amazing work of art. Your very presence is pleasing to Him. He has done and will continue to do miracles in your life. Some will be small things that He does just for you, and no one else sees. Some will be big things that will amaze not only you but everyone around you. As you go through this life, you will see God's handprints all along the way as He guides you on this journey of life. Continue to trust Him with each step. Continue to place your hand in His and watch the beautiful tapestry that will be made. God intricately planned every single moment of your life, and He watches over you as you live each one.

DAY 297

God Is Surrounding You

*"Even when you are chased by those who seek to kill you,
your life is safe in the care of the Lord your God, secure
in his treasure pouch! But the lives of your enemies will
disappear like stones shot from a sling!*
1 Samuel 25:29 NLT

Do not worry about the threats and accusations of the
enemy. He can roar loud, but you have nothing to fear if
you are God's child because he cannot touch you. The
enemy has no new tricks; you will see the same patterns in
everything he does. His battlefield is your mind. The only
power he has in your life is the power you give him in your
mind. His main goal is to separate you from God like he
did Eve by getting you to question God's love and
intentions for you. Always remember he is a liar, and there
is absolutely no truth in him. His day is coming when he
will be completely shut up and wiped away, but until that
day, you are safe with God.

DAY 298

God Is For You

What shall we say about such wonderful things as these?
If God is for us, who can ever be against us?
Romans 8:31 NLT

You do not have to worry about what anyone on this earth thinks about you. God's opinion of you is all that matters. The only relationship in your life that will last for eternity is your relationship with God. He is for you. He will never be against you. He is on your side. Do not try to defend yourself and make people like you. God will defend you. You have His favor. The people who are supposed to be in your life will be. Those who aren't don't try to force relationships with them. Just let them go, and don't try to chase down relationships with people who don't support you and your call. God will bring the right people to walk alongside you on your journey.

DAY 299

God Will Hide You

The Lord is a shelter for the oppressed,
a refuge in times of trouble.
Those who know your name trust in you,
for you, O Lord, do not abandon those
who search for you.
Psalm 9:9-10 NLT

God will never reject you when you run to Him. He is always here for you no matter what you need. He will listen to your prayers and all your worries. God will hide you in the shelter of His wings, safe from your enemies. You can trust Him in every detail. God delights in helping you and taking care of you. Never think that you are forgotten or that you do not matter to God. You are His world. God loves you more than you could ever understand. He will never neglect you or your family. God will always be with you in everything. Holding your hand as you go through pain and turmoil. Rejoicing with you in the good times, mourning with you in the bad times. He is your Father who loves you and wants nothing but good for you.

DAY 300

God Will Shine for You

"No longer will you need the sun to shine by day, nor the moon to give its light by night, for the Lord your God will be your everlasting light, and your God will be your glory. Your sun will never set; your moon will not go down. For the Lord will be your everlasting light. Your days of mourning will come to an end.
Isaiah 60:19-20 NLT

God is the light that guides you by day and by night. Darkness is not dark to Him. He will be your everlasting light that will never go out. When you can't see what is ahead, God will shine for you to see the next step. He will show you the right path to take for your journey. He will walk with you each step of the way. You will never be alone. Even when darkness seems to capture you, God will rescue you and light your way out. No evil can put out God's Light. Before God said let there be light on the earth, He was already shining bright. God is from everlasting to everlasting. The day is coming when all will be encompassed by His light. All your mourning will come to an end. He is the only true Light.

DAY 301

God Is Your Safe Place

I love you, Lord; you are my strength. The Lord is my rock, my fortress, and my savior; my God is my rock, in whom I find protection. He is my shield, the power that saves me, and my place of safety.
Psalm 18:1-2 NLT

God is your protector and defender. You are completely safe with Him. No one can get to you or snatch you from Him. He has a very firm grip on you, and He is not letting you go. God is your Rock, your Fortress, your Strong Tower. He is your Hiding Place. God is the One you can run to for protection. He is your Father, and He watches over you with careful eyes. His shield wraps around you and covers you. He will always run to your rescue. God is your place of safety. Put your life in His hands, not the hands of man. No army on earth can protect you and defend you like God can. He has legions of angels ready at His word to protect you from your enemies and save you from danger. You can fall into Him, and He will keep you safe.

DAY 302

Lead Others To God

*Meanwhile, the priests who were carrying the Ark of the
Lord's Covenant stood on dry ground in the middle of the
riverbed as the people passed by. They waited there until
the whole nation of Israel had crossed the Jordan
on dry ground.*
Joshua 3:17 NLT

Once God has set you free and caused you to walk across
the Jordan on dry ground, it is time for you to lead others
across the Jordan. Do not leave them alone. You are to
guide them to Him. He will use your life, and you will be
a priest that will carry His presence. God's presence goes
with you everywhere you go, and that presence will draw
others to you. Stay with them until they have crossed onto
dry ground, and then they will become a priest to carry His
presence and help others across their Jordan. God comforts
you and delivers you so that you can comfort and help
others find deliverance. You cannot deliver them, but you
can lead them to God so that He can deliver them. Never
make yourself their savior. Only lead them to Him.

DAY 303

Your Enemies Are Surrounded By God

*When the servant of the man of God rose early in the
morning and went out, behold, an army with horses and
chariots was all around the city. And the servant said,
"Alas, my master! What shall we do?" He said, "Do not
be afraid, for those who are with us are more than those
who are with them." Then Elisha prayed and said, "O
Lord, please open his eyes that he may see." So the Lord
opened the eyes of the young man, and he saw, and
behold, the mountain was full of horses and chariots of
fire all around Elisha.*
2 Kings 6:16-17 ESV

Sometimes in the middle of a battle, when it feels like you
are surrounded and have no way out, you will begin to be
afraid, but these are the times when you must look with
spiritual eyes and see the truth. You may feel surrounded
by your enemies but remember that your enemies are
surrounded by God. He controls everything you go
through, and He sets boundaries that your enemy cannot
cross. His angels are always on guard to protect you and
keep you. You will not be defeated if you look with
spiritual eyes and keep your trust in Him. He has you
tucked away in His secret place. God has got you. Do not
be afraid.

DAY 304

Forever In God's Hands & Heart

From the ends of the earth, I cry to you for help when my heart is overwhelmed. Lead me to the towering rock of safety, for you are my safe refuge, a fortress where my enemies cannot reach me. Let me live forever in your sanctuary, safe beneath the shelter of your wings!
Psalm 61:2-4 NLT

Immediately when God hears your cry for help, He reaches down to rescue you. When your heart is overwhelmed, and you feel you can't go on, He will be your strength. He is your rock of safety. He will never leave you alone or forsake you. God will never fail you when you need Him. The enemy cannot touch you in His hands. You are completely safe with God. He hides you forever under the shelter of His wings. God loves you, and He is careful with you. He guards you and watches over you to keep you on the right path and out of the way of harm. Keep your eyes on Him and your ears tuned to His voice. He will lead you and guide you to your destination safely. You are forever in God's hands and forever in His heart.

DAY 305

He Alone Is God

First I predicted your rescue,
then I saved you and proclaimed it to the world.
No foreign god has ever done this.
You are witnesses that I am the only God,"
says the Lord. "From eternity to eternity I am God.
No one can snatch anyone out of my hand.
No one can undo what I have done."
Isaiah 43:12-13 NLT

You know Him as God because He chose to reveal Himself to you. He chose you before you ever took a breath on the earth. He already knew you, knew everything about you.

God knew every decision you would make, and He prepared for that. He planned long before you ever spoke His name. God is the One who has carried you along and taken care of you every time you needed help. Only God can truly rescue you, save you, and set you free. He has you in His very capable hands, and He will not drop you. No one can ever snatch you from His hands. He will not let anyone harm you. He has a marvelous plan for your life, and He will bring it to pass, and no one can stop it, and no one can reverse it. He is God alone!

DAY 306

You Will Be Victorious

The one thing I ask of the Lord—
the thing I seek most—is to live in the house of
the Lord all the days of my life, delighting in the Lord's
perfections and meditating in his Temple. For he will
conceal me there when troubles come; he will hide me in
his sanctuary. He will place me out of reach on a high
rock. Then I will hold my head high above my enemies
who surround me. At his sanctuary I will offer sacrifices
with shouts of joy, singing and praising the Lord with
music.
Psalm 27:4-6 NLT

God wants to be your one thing. He wants you seek Him above all else. He won't force you to do this. You will never regret it. Things will go better for you in this life if you are living with God as the center of everything you do and every decision you make. He will be with you in trouble and rescue you and honor you. He will pour His favor out upon you so that even in bad times, you will be blessed. Everyone around you will know that you are His because of the things He will do in your life when you make Him first. God will hold you out of the reach of your enemies and set you high upon a rock. You will be victorious in what you put your hands to. He will put His praise on your lips, and you will shout His name to all the earth.

DAY 307

You Will Not Be Overtaken

They will fight you, but they will fail. For I am with you,
and I will take care of you. I, the Lord, have spoken!"
Jeremiah 1:19 NLT

No weapon that is formed against you will prosper. This means that your enemies will try to hurt you. The weapons will be formed, but because you are God's, the weapons will not prosper against you. They can try all they want, but if you stick with Him, your enemies will not triumph over you. God is with you everywhere you go and in everything you do. He does not ever take His eyes off you. He wraps you in His shield of protection. He is your front and rear guard. Like a helicopter parent, God is always around you. He loves you, and He will not let anyone take you out of His protection, ever. You can sleep at night and wake up in the morning knowing that your Father is fighting for you. His love for you is fierce. He will not allow you to be overtaken.

DAY 308

God Will Come Through

*As soon as I pray, you answer me;
you encourage me by giving me strength.*
Psalm 138:3 NLT

God's ears are always open and aware, listening for your voice. The moment He hears you cry out; He goes into action to help you. He will always answer you. You may not like His answer sometimes, it may not look like you want it to, or come when you want it to, but He will always answer. While you wait, He will be your strength. God will give you breath when you feel like you can't breathe because it hurts too bad. He will encourage you, and His peace will wash over you. He will give you the courage to go on another day. God will provide you with the determination to not give up. He will give you the faith to believe that He will come through.

DAY 309

Commit Everything To God

*Commit your actions to the Lord,
and your plans will succeed.*
Proverbs 16:3 NLT

When you commit all your plans to God, He will help you. Remember that sometimes your plans are not His plans, though, so always hold them loosely because He may change them. If you have prayed and know that what you are about to do is something that God has told you to do, you can move forward with confidence, knowing that He will put His favor and protection on your plans, and they will succeed. It is foolish to set out to do something that you have not consulted with God on and then be upset when it doesn't work out. He is in control of everything, and He loves you and wants the best for you, so He wants you to ask Him, and He will help you to make wise and Godly plans in all you do. God will give you the grace and strength you need to carry out those plans.

DAY 310

All Will Go Well

Oh, fear the Lord, you his saints, for those who fear him have no lack! The young lions suffer want and hunger but those who seek the Lord lack no good thing.
Psalm 34:9-10 ESV

Your worship and awe are what God wants. When you worship Him in awe and wonder, you will lack nothing. God will make sure that everything in your life is complete. You will never go without the things you need. God will care for you and your family. He will surround you with His love and protection. He will make His light shine on you all the days of your life. God does not want you to fear Him in a way that says He will harm you, but fear simply means you respect Him, worship Him, stand in awe of Him, knowing there is no other god but Him. When you do this, all will be well with your soul.

DAY 311

God's Love For You

*But I trust in your unfailing love. I will rejoice because
you have rescued me. I will sing to the Lord
because he is good to me.*
Psalm 13:5-6 NLT

If you could only know how much God loves you. His love for you would go to the ends of the earth to find you. His love for you reaches higher than the highest heavens. God's love for you is beyond the most fantastic imaginations. It is like nothing you have ever experienced. When you truly know God's love for you, you will want for nothing. You will know you are complete. You will have a solid foundation that nothing can move or shake. God's love is the most powerful force on earth. His love sent Jesus to a cross just for you. When His love touches your life and mind, you will never be the same. God loves YOU!

DAY 312

Tell Them

The Lord is not slow to fulfill his promise as some count slowness, but is patient toward you, not wishing that any should perish, but that all should reach repentance.
2 Peter 3:9 ESV

God does not want anyone to perish. He desires everyone to know of His love for them, that is why He is taking so long to make everything new and bring you to where He is. God needs you to help Him tell others of His great love and grace. He wants you to tell your story and point them to Him so that He can rescue them just as He has rescued you.

Remember when you were lost, and someone pointed you to God, and He loved you and forgave all your sins? Tell that to them. Tell of the times He has wrapped you in His arms and comforted you. Tell them of the times He has healed you and delivered you when no one else knew how to help you. Tell them how He took away your shame and gave you a new identity and a new life. Tell them so that they will be with us when the earth passes away and you come to where God is.

DAY 313

You Love Because God Loved

We love each other because he loved us first.
If someone says, "I love God," but hates a fellow
believer, that person is a liar; for if we don't love people
we can see, how can we love God, whom we cannot see?
1 John 4:19-20 NLT

God is love. Without knowing God and His love for you, you can never really know what true love is. You cannot pour love into others without God first pouring His love into you. It is a continuous cycle. As He loves you, you love others. If a person says they love God but go around being cruel to others and have no compassion, you know that person does not even know God or His love. If they say they love God but don't help the hurting and turn a blind eye to those in need, they do not have His love in them. How can they love God when they can't even love those who are right in front of them? You will know those who truly love God and truly have Him living in them by how they treat the people standing right in front of them.

DAY 314

It's The Little Things

Catch all the foxes,
those little foxes, before they ruin the vineyard of love,
for the grapevines are blossoming!
Song of Songs 2:15 NLT

Be careful of the small things you allow into your mind, which eventually get into your heart. Those tiny little habits that you shrug off as nothing big or important. Satan knows that if he can keep giving you the tiny lies, keep you believing those little things don't hurt, then piece by piece, he can infiltrate your relationship with God until the tiny things eventually become big things and you didn't even realize it was happening. Ask God to show you those things and He will, and then ask Him to help you remove those things, and He will. Together you can overcome anything. Satan is no match for you and God. Just don't ignore those things any longer.

DAY 315

Benefits Of Being God's

May the Lord bless you and protect you. May the Lord smile on you and be gracious to you. May the Lord show you his favor and give you his peace.
Numbers 6:24-26 NLT

God's blessings are always on your life because you are His child, and He loves you. His protection is constantly surrounding you. God goes before you and behind you. He is above you and below you. His presence surrounds you and knits you in. He is pleased with you always. He smiles at the thought of you. He loves to be gracious to you. God's grace gives you things that you don't deserve, but it also empowers you to do something that you could never do on your own. Show this grace to others also. His favor follows you everywhere you go. It goes before you with every person in every situation. God's peace envelops you right when you need it. It keeps you calm when you should be chaotic. It goes beyond anything you could ever understand. Because you are His child, you walk in these things daily. Greater than anything is God's love for you. Because of it, Jesus shed His blood for you so you could have a relationship with nothing ever separating you again.

DAY 316

Don't Look Back

This is what God says the God who builds a road right through the ocean, who carves a path through pounding waves, The God who summons horses and chariots and armies— they lie down and then can't get up; they're snuffed out like so many candles: "Forget about what's happened; don't keep going over old history. Be alert, be present. I'm about to do something brand-new. It's bursting out! Don't you see it? There it is!
Isaiah 43:16-19 MSG

God wants you to forget everything that has happened in the past. No more looking back; you are only looking to what is happening now and in the future. Be alert and ready when God asks you to move. He is working in your life and around you to do something new and amazing. He is weaving a beautiful tapestry together. It is already happening if you pay attention, even in the small details God is at work. Remember that nothing is impossible for Him. He is the One who caused the Israelites to walk through the sea on dry ground and then buried their enemies under it. Get ready! Keep your eyes on God. It won't be long now, and the dam that has stood in front of you will burst open. Don't be afraid of what you must leave behind because what is ahead is so much better!

DAY 317

Do Not Be Afraid

The Lord is my light and my salvation—so why should I be afraid? The Lord is my fortress, protecting me from danger, so why should I tremble?
Psalm 27:1 NLT

You have nothing to fear because He is your God. God is your loving, kind, and protective Father. He will always run to rescue you. God's presence is always with you and in you. He is your light to guide your way on this journey of life. He will always answer when you call His name. God's love for you is fierce and will take on any enemy. He is the God of all creation; nothing is impossible for Him. He can make a way where there is no way. He can shut the mouths of lions and walk with you through the fire, and you will not even be touched. Put your trust in Him. Put your trust in His love for you. God's eyes are always on you. You are never far away from Him. He is not a distant God watching what happens; He is involved. He is personal to you. Do not be afraid; He will take care of you.

DAY 318

The Gift Of Peace

*"I am leaving you with a gift—peace of mind and heart.
And the peace I give is a gift the world cannot give. So
don't be troubled or afraid.*
John 14:27 NLT

God's peace is unlike anything you could ever imagine on
this earth. His peace goes way beyond your reasoning and
understanding. He is the Prince of Peace. When you have
Him in your life, you have perfect peace that guards your
heart and mind. He is your Perfect Peace. His peace is like
a warm wave that washes over you and calms all your
worries and anxieties. You can walk in this peace when
you understand how much God loves you and want good
for you. He will be here for you and take perfect care of
you. When you know this, you can sit back and relax and
rest in His arms, knowing that He has everything under
control. Even in the middle of the most severe storms, you
can have this peace. It is a gift for His children. You cannot
earn it by something you do. Just trust Him. Fix your eyes
and your thoughts on God.

DAY 319

God Will Make You Holy & Blameless

Now may the God of peace make you holy in every way,
and may your whole spirit and soul and body be kept
blameless until our Lord Jesus Christ comes again. God
will make this happen, for he who calls you is faithful.
1 Thessalonians 5:23-24 NLT

You cannot make yourself holy before God. You cannot save yourself or make yourself better so that He will save you. From beginning to end, holiness and salvation are God's doing. He makes you holy and blameless and gives you peace. Nothing in this world can save you. You can't read your Bible or go to church enough to save yourself. Your mom or dad can't save you. Only God can do this for you. He has already made a way for you to be holy and blameless through the blood of Jesus. There is no other way to God except through Jesus. When you believe in Him and accept Him into your life, it gives you access to God because His blood washes you as pure as snow.

God is the one who chose you and draws you to Himself. Him, not you. It is all about Him and the finished work of the cross. All you need to do is believe!

DAY 320

Because Of Who He Is

For the Lord is good.
His unfailing love continues forever,
and his faithfulness continues to each generation.
Psalm 100:5 NLT

God is a good Father. He is always good, and He always does good. There is no evil within Him. There is no darkness around Him. He is light. He is a loving Father. God loves you more than you will ever be able to comprehend. His love goes beyond the most amazing thing on this earth. He is so, so kind and compassionate. He wants to help you and take care of you. God has the best of intentions at heart toward you. He is always faithful; even when you doubt and question, it does not change His faithfulness. Nothing you do can change who He is. You can trust His love and His intentions toward you. He will forever keep the promises He has made to you. You will see them come to pass. None of this depends on you. It is all because of who He is. Because He loves you with all His heart. He will never let you down.

DAY 321

Expect Your Freedom

O Israel, hope in the Lord!
For with the Lord there is steadfast love,
and with him is plentiful redemption.
Psalm 130:7 ESV

Never give up on God. Never give up on the dreams that He has placed in your heart. Always hope; hope is an anchor for your soul. Always trust; trust causes you to be able to rest and wait patiently on Him. Always remember that He loves you more than you can imagine and that He is kind toward you. Do not give up hope that you will taste your freedom while you are here in the land of the living. God has unlimited resources to make it happen. He is not limited by any boundaries that the natural world is limited by. He created everything out of nothing, and He can do it again if He needs to for you. God is above and beyond anything you could imagine, and He can do above and beyond even your wildest dreams. Expect Him to come through for you. Celebrate before you see the answer because He will do what He has promised you He would do. You will taste and know that He is good. You will see your deliverance. Just stand still, be calm and wait on Him.

DAY 322

Simply By Faith

Because of our faith, Christ has brought us into this place
of undeserved privilege where we now stand, and we
confidently and joyfully look forward
to sharing God's glory.
Romans 5:2 NLT

It is by pure faith that you are saved and brought into God's grace. There is nothing you can do to earn it. You cannot boast about how good you are or how smart you are. You cannot buy your way in. Simply by believing in Jesus Christ and His finished work on the cross, you receive salvation. His sacrifice was enough; there is nothing you can do to add to it. Nothing needs to be added to it; it is perfect. This is His story, not your story, but He wants you to be a part of His story and see His glory. His grace is entirely undeserved and completely free. All you need to do is simply believe.

DAY 323

Thrilled With You

Behold, you are beautiful, my love;
behold, you are beautiful;
your eyes are doves.
Song of Solomon 1:15 ESV

You are so very lovely to God. You are His masterpiece.
He is enthralled with you, His child. His heart leaps at the
sound of your voice. God loved planning for you and then
watching as you were woven together intricately bit by bit
in your mother's womb. He was delighted when you took
your first breath, and He heard your first cry. Like a proud
dad, He was beaming from ear to ear. You were not an
accident. You were planned for before the foundations of
the earth were laid. God loves when you come and share
your heart with Him. He is excited when you ask Him for
help in your life. God loves to show up in a big way and
amaze you. It delights Him to give you good things and
watch His purpose unfold in your life. God is so totally in
love with you, His child.

DAY 324

Unharmed & Unbound

But suddenly, Nebuchadnezzar jumped up in amazement and exclaimed to his advisers, "Didn't we tie up three men and throw them into the furnace?" "Yes, Your Majesty, we certainly did," they replied. "Look!" Nebuchadnezzar shouted. "I see four men, unbound, walking around in the fire unharmed! And the fourth looks like a god!"
Daniel 3:24-25 NLT

Even when you are thrown into a fire, you will not walk through it alone. God will be right there beside you, walking with you. The fire will have no lasting effects on you. The only thing the fire is going to do is serve to set you free. You will walk out of the fire better off than you were when you went in. You will come out stronger and even closer to God. When you walk out of the fiery furnace, you will walk out unharmed and unbound. The fire will burn off the chains that had you in bondage. People around you will be amazed when you emerge and know without a doubt that your God is the one true God!

DAY 325

God Made You To Love

The Lord did not set his heart on you and choose you because you were more numerous than other nations, for you were the smallest of all nations!
Deuteronomy 7:7 NLT

God did not choose you because of how good you are, how smart you are, how rich you are, or how beautiful you are. He chose you because He wanted to, because He loves you. He chose you before you ever took a breath. You cannot earn His approval or His acceptance. Everything you receive from Him is because His love for you sent Jesus to a cross for you so that you and He could have a relationship. By that relationship, you have become His child, and as His child, you receive all His blessings and affections freely. There is absolutely nothing you can do to make Him love you and want you more or make Him love you and want you less. His love for you is complete because of who He is. God is love. He cannot do anything except love you. He made you to love before you ever lifted a finger for Him or even said His name. Just rest in that love.

DAY 326

Triumphantly Face Your Foes

They do not fear bad news; they confidently trust the Lord to care for them. They are confident and fearless and can face their foes triumphantly.
Psalm 112:7-8 NLT

You can come to a place of rest and trust in God to the point that you do not even fear when bad news comes. You have peace even amid crisis because you know who your Father is, and you know that He will take perfect care of you. When the storms of life come to blow you down, you can walk confidently with your head held high through them. You can be fearless as you face all your enemies because you know that through Christ, you are an overcomer. You already walk in complete victory even before it manifest. You are not a cowering fearful slave, but you are a child of the Most High God. The Commander of Angel Armies is your Father; you have absolutely nothing to fear.

DAY 327

Not One Word Unfulfilled

*And the Lord said, "That's right, and it means that I am
watching, and I will certainly carry out all my plans."*
Jeremiah 1:12 NLT

Not one word that God has spoken to you will go
unfulfilled. If He has given you a promise, you can plant
your feet on it. His promises are not based on you. They
are based on His faithfulness and the fact that He is
trustworthy and able. You never have to try to fulfill a
promise that He gives you on your own. When you try to
bring about His promises in your time and your way, it will
eventually end in disaster, frustration, and confusion. Trust
His ways and His timing. You don't need to know all the
details. You don't need to be able to see how it will happen.
All you need to do is believe it will happen and trust God
with everything else. You see with natural eyes and think
there is no way, but God sees things you don't see, and He
work in the realms of the Spirit where natural eyes are no
use. He has methods that are entirely unknown to you.
Remember that His ways are always perfect. He tailor
makes plans and promises just for you. All God needs you
to do is trust and move when He tells you to.

DAY 328

God Is Greater

And every spirit that does not confess Jesus is not from God. This is the spirit of the antichrist, which you heard was coming and now is in the world already. Little children, you are from God and have overcome them, for he who is in you is greater than he who is in the world.
1 John 4:3-4 ESV

You do not have to worry about the evil one who prowls around this earth looking for people to devour. You are God's child, and because of the blood of Jesus, He now lives fully inside of you through the Holy Spirit. He is greater than anything you could ever face on this earth. There is no demon in hell that can overcome you when you are full of God's Spirit. No sickness can take you out. No bondage can hold you bound. No addiction can capture you. He will fight for you. Trust your life in His capable hands. God is with you, and He is in you, and He has given you authority over all the power of the enemy. Your enemy must bow to God's Spirit living in you. Take heart, be bold, have courage; the Greater One abides in you.

DAY 329

Embrace God's Way

This is why the fulfillment of God's promise depends entirely on trusting God and his way, and then simply embracing him and what he does. God's promise arrives as pure gift. That's the only way everyone can be sure to get in on it, those who keep the religious traditions and those who have never heard of them. For Abraham is father of us all. He is not our racial father—that's reading the story backward. He is our faith father.
Romans 4:16 MSG

God's promises to you are a gift that you get through the finished work of Jesus, simply because He loves you and has a plan for you and wants to be good to you. His promises are not based on you checking off all the boxes, dotting all the i's, and crossing all the t's. It isn't about keeping all the religious traditions and never making a mistake. The fulfillment of His promises are based on you trusting Him, not on you working hard enough to earn them or being good enough to get them. It is simply believing that He will do what He said He would do. It is about letting go of your control and embracing God's ways and God's timing. Don't make it harder than it must be, simply believe. Believe that He is good and that His ways are perfect. Believe that His love for you is unfailing and faithful. Believe that God wants nothing but the absolute best for you.

DAY 330

Steady As You Go

*I waited patiently for the Lord to help me, and he turned
to me and heard my cry. He lifted me out of the pit of
despair, out of the mud and the mire. He set my feet on
solid ground and steadied me as I walked along. He has
given me a new song to sing, a hymn of praise to our
God. Many will see what he has done and be amazed.
They will put their trust in the Lord.*
Psalm 40:1-3 NLT

Wait patiently for God. He will not disappoint you. He
hears every prayer you pray, even the ones that you don't
say out loud. He will lift you up out of the deepest darkest
pit, even if you got yourself into it. He will set your feet on
the solid foundation of His love for you, and He will steady
you as you walk the path of purpose that He has already
laid out for you. He will not throw you out into something
that you are not ready for. Each step prepares you for the
next. Don't be in a hurry and walk in front of Him. He will
put a new song of praise in your heart when you see what
He has done in your life. You will be so amazed at the
plans He has for you. Not only will you be amazed, but
also all the ones watching or hearing your story. They will
see His work in your life, and they will put their trust in
Him. Wait for God.

DAY 331

Write It Down

And the Lord answered me: "Write the vision; make it plain on tablets, so he may run who reads it. For still the vision awaits its appointed time; it hastens to the end—it will not lie. If it seems slow, wait for it; it will surely come; it will not delay.
Habakkuk 2:2-3 ESV

Write down the dreams God has given you. Tuck them away in your heart. Even when it looks like they will never come to fruition, don't give up on them. He is constantly working behind the scenes to maneuver things on your behalf. He is working to bring the right opportunities, to open the right doors, and to bring the right people alongside you at the exact right time. More importantly, God is preparing you for what He has prepared for you so that when you arrive at the fulfillment of the dream, you will be ready and not crumble under the pressure of it. God is building intimacy and a relationship with you, so you will depend on Him and not your own strength. When the fulfillment arrives, you need to know that it is Him that sustains you. Don't carry the weight of it on your shoulders. It will indeed be fulfilled. It will be at the appointed time and not a moment late.

DAY 332

He Named The Stars

Look up into the heavens.
Who created all the stars? He brings them out like an
army, one after another,
calling each by its name. Because of his great power
and incomparable strength, not a single one is missing.
Isaiah 40:26 NLT

God is the one who placed all the stars in the sky. He counted them all and called each one by name. He put the planets into their places. When you are worried and don't see a way, look up at the stars and know that you mean more to Him than every single one of those stars. Remember that the same God who flung all those stars into the sky and placed the planets into orbit is your Father and loves you madly. He created everything you see with your eyes now out of nothing. There is nothing too difficult for Him. He is God, and there is no other. From beginning to end, it is Him. Before time, He was. After time ends, He will be. God is with you, and He loves you.

DAY 333

Rest

*For I have given rest to the weary
and joy to the sorrowing.*
Jeremiah 31:25 NLT

Allow yourself to rest. It is okay not to have everything figured out. It is okay not to know what is ahead sometimes. It is okay not to get everything done. Stop, and let your soul, your mind, and your body rest. Crawl up in God's lap and lean into Him and let all the worries and cares of the world melt away. If you do not rest on your own will, your body and mind will eventually make you rest because you will wear yourself out. God rested after creating the world to show you that it is proper to rest. You need to rest physically, but you also need to rest mentally. If you are mentally tired, it affects every other area of your body also. Your body, mind, and spirit are so interconnected together and function with each other. It is so important to take care of each one. God gives you permission to rest.

DAY 334

Bring To Completion

The Lord will fulfill his purpose for me;
your steadfast love, O Lord, endures forever.
Do not forsake the work of your hands.
Psalm 138:8 ESV

God will not begin something in you and not bring it to completion. When He does a work, He does not leave anything untouched. You will have nothing missing and nothing lacking. He will take care of your body, mind, and spirit. God will always do what He has promised you He would do. Even if everyone else has lied to you and broken their promises, you can trust God that He will not. God cannot lie. He will care for you all the days of your life. He will continue to pour out His unfailing love on you. You will never have to walk this journey of life alone. God is with you now, and He will be with you for eternity to come.

DAY 335

Trust What God Can Do

We call Abraham "father" not because he got God's attention by living like a saint, but because God made something out of Abraham when he was a nobody. Isn't that what we've always read in Scripture, God saying to Abraham, "I set you up as father of many peoples"? Abraham was first named "father" and then became a father because he dared to trust God to do what only God could do: raise the dead to life, with a word make something out of nothing. When everything was hopeless, Abraham believed anyway, deciding to live not on the basis of what he saw he couldn't do but on what God said he would do. And so he was made father of a multitude of peoples. God himself said to him, "You're going to have a big family, Abraham!"
Romans 4:17-18 MSG

God called Abraham a father before he ever became a father. He believed that God would do what He said He would do. God took Abraham from obscurity to being the father of the nations. Abraham received his promise, not because he was so good, but because he trusted God to do what only He could do. Abraham knew that if God said He would do something, He would do it. He knew that God could raise the dead and create something out of nothing, so he knew God could make him a father in his old age.

He believed in God's promises and who God is more than he trusted in the circumstances in front of him. He didn't live out of what he knew he couldn't do, but out of what God said He would do, and this is how you can receive your promises too. Trust in God and His promises to you. Trust in who He is, not in the circumstances in front of you or what you can or cannot do.

DAY 336

No More Shame

And since we have a great High Priest who rules over God's house, let us go right into the presence of God with sincere hearts fully trusting him. For our guilty consciences have been sprinkled with Christ's blood to make us clean, and our bodies have been washed with pure water.
Hebrews 10:21-22 NLT

You can come into God's presence without fear, trusting that He loves you and He is kind and gentle. You no longer must live your life in guilt and shame, always wondering if He is pleased with you. Because of the blood of Jesus, He will always be pleased with you. When you sin, it doesn't cause Him to be angry at you or want to smite you or throw you away. No matter what, when He looks at you because you are under the blood of Jesus and you are now His child, He sees you as pure and clean. You have been washed as white as snow. You don't have to hide anything from God. He already knows all you do and think, but He loves you anyway. His love for you is so much deeper and wider and higher than any sin you commit. Run to God boldly and receive His forgiveness and mercy quickly. Do not hold your head down in shame; you are His, and He has redeemed you.

DAY 337

Be Excited

Have I not commanded you? Be strong and courageous.
Do not be frightened, and do not be dismayed, for the
Lord your God is with you wherever you go."
Joshua 1:9 ESV

God will go with you everywhere you go. Do not be afraid
when He sends you to places that you have never been. Be
excited about the adventure and know that He is with you
every moment. Be strong and courageous in this journey
you are on. Be bold and stand tall when you are fulfilling
the call on your life, no matter what that looks like. No one
can harm you. God will protect you on all sides. He has
legions of angels at His command to take care of you. He
is your Father, and He controls everything. With one
breath, He can create whatever He wants to. With the flick
of one finger, He can change things. Nothing is too hard
for God. Just be obedient to whatever He tells you to do,
and He will take care of everything else. Keep your eyes
on Him. Be excited about the journey, do not be afraid.

DAY 338

God Is Building You

*"Stand at attention while I prepare you for your work.
I'm making you as impregnable as a castle, Immovable as
a steel post, solid as a concrete block wall. You're a one-
man defense system against this culture, Against Judah's
kings and princes, against the priests and local leaders.
They'll fight you, but they won't even scratch you. I'll
back you up every inch of the way." God's Decree.*
Jeremiah 1:18-19 MSG

God has called you by your name and wants to use you for
His Kingdom. He is making you strong and preparing you
for what is ahead for you. He will fortify you inside and
out. He will put His strength in your inner man. Your
enemies will try, but they will not prosper against you. God
will keep you safe within His secret place. You will stand
against the lies and deceit of the culture you are in. You
will help people to remove the veil from their eyes and see
the truth. God will be with you, so you never have to be
afraid. He will cause His light to shine upon you, and many
will see that it is Him who works in you and through you.

DAY 339

His Love Makes A Way

He brought me out into a broad place;
he rescued me, because he delighted in me.
Psalm 18:19 ESV

God's love for you will kick down walls, open doors, and move mountains. His love is the most powerful force there is. It was His love that sent Jesus to a cross to open a way for you to step into the Holy Place with Him and have a relationship. God's love takes you to a place you have never ever been before. A place that is free from bondage and oppression into a wide-open and beautiful life. A life that is lived close to Him. Wrapped in His presence. You can come to Him with your needs for yourself, you don't need a priest to come for you. Now the veil has been torn from top to bottom, and your sin has been wiped away; nothing can ever separate us again. It was God's delight to do this for you because He delights in you.

DAY 340

God Looks At The Heart

But the Lord said to Samuel, "Don't judge by his appearance or height, for I have rejected him. The Lord doesn't see things the way you see them. People judge by outward appearance, but the Lord looks at the heart."
1 Samuel 16:7 NLT

God does not look at the outward appearance of people. The people that this world would write off as foolish and weak, those are the ones He choose for His Kingdom's work. God does not want someone who thinks they have it all together or thinks they know it all. He needs someone with a humble heart who will obey what He asks them to do and not have to be in control. Take heart because even if everyone on earth says you can't do it or aren't good enough. If everyone else counts you out, that is good because God chooses you. You were never meant to fit into this world. You were meant to fit into His Kingdom. He has His hand on your life, and He calls you chosen.

DAY 341

God Gives You Clarity

*For I will set My eyes on them for good, and I will bring
them back to this land; I will build them and not
pull them down, and I will plant them and not
pluck them up.*
Jeremiah 24:6 NKJV

God's intentions for you are always good. He is always
looking for ways to be good to you. When you have been
in a storm for a long time, you get weary and sometimes
start to wander into places you wouldn't usually go. The
storm can skew your view and cause you to see things
differently, but He will bring you back after the storm has
passed to a place where you are steady, and your vision is
clear again. You become weak in the storm, but He will
build you back up and restore you better than you were
before. He will plant your feet in His love for you, and you
will be on solid ground. You will not be blown back and
forth in the next storm that comes along. He will be your
firm foundation.

DAY 342

Small Steps Matter

*Then another message came to me from the Lord:
"Zerubbabel is the one who laid the foundation of this
Temple, and he will complete it. Then you will know that
the Lord of Heaven's Armies has sent me. Do not despise
these small beginnings, for the Lord rejoices to see the
work begin, to see the plumb line in Zerubbabel's hand."*
Zechariah 4:8-10 NLT

Do not despise the small things. Celebrate the small steps,
even if they are baby steps. Each step leads to something
bigger until you have made it to where you are going. The
small victories all add up to a big victory. God celebrates
when He sees you take even the tiniest step forward. Don't
wait until you have reached your goal to celebrate and be
joyful, do it all along the way! God started this work in
you, and He will finish it, but you need to be moving
forward each day. There will be times when others don't
celebrate with you, and that is okay; God will celebrate
with you. There are times when no one even knows you
took the step, but He knows, and He is proud of you when
you do. God knows that sometimes even that tiny step you
took was more challenging for you than you showed on the
outside. He sees those steps. One day you will look back
and realize that to God, all those tiny steps were significant
because each time you stepped, He moved mountains for
you.

DAY 343

Do Unto Others

*"Because the poor are plundered, because the needy
groan, I will now arise," says the Lord;
"I will place him in the safety for which he longs."*
Psalm 12:5 ESV

God is a God who loves justice and will always defend those who cannot defend themselves. He will do this for you. He will defend you when you are defenseless. God will provide for you when you are poor. He will deliver you when you are oppressed. He will help you when you are needy. God will always surround you and protect you. He will rescue you from all your enemies. Because God loves you, He will do this for you. God wants you to do for others what He does for you. Feed the hungry, clothe the poor, take care of widows and orphans. Guide the oppressed to Him for deliverance. Sometimes it seems as if God is doing nothing, but He is moving upon the hearts of man to be His hands and feet. He needs your obedience to help those around you as He helps you.

DAY 344

Not A Slave To Fear

This resurrection life you received from God is not a timid, grave-tending life. It's adventurously expectant, greeting God with a childlike "What's next, Papa?" God's Spirit touches our spirits and confirms who we really are. We know who he is, and we know who we are: Father and children. And we know we are going to get what's coming to us—an unbelievable inheritance! We go through exactly what Christ goes through. If we go through the hard times with him, then we're certainly going to go through the good times with him!
Romans 8:15-17 MSG

You are not a cowering fearful slave; you are a child of the Most High God! He will confirm this to you as many times as you need Him too. God wants you to walk in this confidence every day in every situation. He wants you to come to understand who He is and who you are in Him. Spend time with Him and get to know His character and hear God whisper your identity to you. Because you are His child, you can be sure that your future will be promising. There are so many good things waiting for you both here in this life and when you leave this life and come home with Him. You will have bad times, but God will be with you in them, and there will be so many good times. He will go through the good and the bad hand in hand with you. Do not fear because you are God's.

DAY 345

Complete Healing

*I will give you back your health and heal your wounds,"
says the Lord. "For you are called an
outcast— 'Jerusalem for whom no one cares.'"*
Jeremiah 30:17 NLT

Come to God, and He will help you. Jesus took the stripes
on His back for your healing. This includes physical,
mental, emotional, and spiritual healing. God is always
willing to heal you, but you must remember it may not
come in the way you want it to or look like you want it to.
There may be specific instructions that He gives you, just
as He told Naaman to wash in the Jordan River seven
times, and it didn't make sense, but he obeyed and was
healed. Just keep your ears open to what He tells you.
Sometimes His healing comes instantly, but sometimes it
is a process.

However God chooses to heal you, trust Him. Just like
physical wounds take time to heal, so do mental and
emotional wounds. We must clean them out and bandage
them up and allow them time to heal. Healing happens
from the inside out. God loves you, and He wants to heal
you and make you whole.

DAY 346

God Has A Firm Grip

I, your God, have a firm grip on you and I'm not letting go. I'm telling you, 'Don't panic. I'm right here to help you.'
Isaiah 41:13 MSG

God is holding you tight. You are never ever alone. You can trust that He has a firm grip on you, and He is not letting you go for anything or anyone. No power of hell can snatch you away from Him or cause Him to let you go. He will not drop you. He will always hold tightly to you. You do not ever need to panic or fear because He is right here with you. God will always be right here beside you to help you. Just call His name, and He will come running to rescue you. God guards you and puts a wall of protection around you that no enemy can ever penetrate. You are hemmed in on all sides.

Rest in God's love for you, knowing that nothing is impossible for Him, and He will always take complete and perfect care of you.

DAY 347

God Will Show You The Way

Let me hear of your unfailing love each morning, for I am trusting you. Show me where to walk, for I give myself to you.
Psalm 143:8 NLT

When you give yourself to God completely, He will take care of you. He will show you the path to take for your life. Everyone's journey will look different, so do not compare your journey to anyone else's. Go to God for wisdom for each step you take, don't run to a man to find out the plan for your life. Your destination is unique to the plans He has made for you. Keep your eyes on God and not on what everyone else around you is doing. He will take you on the best path. There may be bumps along the way, but He will be with you and guide you even through the bumps. His unfailing love will follow you each step of the way. Just keep trusting God each day for the road ahead.

DAY 348

God Is Your Hope

But the Lord watches over those who fear him,
those who rely on his unfailing love.
He rescues them from death
and keeps them alive in times of famine.
We put our hope in the Lord.
He is our help and our shield.
Psalm 33:18-20 NLT

No matter what you see in front of you, do not fear. God's children live by faith in Him, not by sight. No matter what your circumstances are screaming at you, trust God. He will come through for you. Expect Him to show up and do good for you and towards you. Never lose your hope; it is an anchor for your faith. God will deliver you and honor you. He will help you in times of trouble. You will never lack the things you need. God will make a way where you see no way. Put your hope in God, and your face will be radiant with joy. There will be no shame for those who hope and trust in God. His love for you will be your firm foundation, and He will wrap Himself around you and give you strength.

DAY 349

Beautifully Broken

The Lord will comfort Israel again
and have pity on her ruins.
Her desert will blossom like Eden,
her barren wilderness like the garden of the Lord.
Joy and gladness will be found there.
Songs of thanksgiving will fill the air.
Isaiah 51:3 NLT

God brings restoration and redemption to those He loves.
God will put back together every broken part of you. Your
brokenness brings beauty to your life. It gives you intimacy
with Him and compassion for others. It is out of your
brokenness that God can put you back together in a whole
new way.

God will transform you into something beautiful from the
inside out. You will walk from your time of being
beautifully broken with joy and laughter in your heart and
on your lips. So many lives will be changed because of
your willingness to embrace the broken pieces and allow
God to heal them. You will walk away with a thankful
heart and a new song on your lips.

DAY 350

God Defends & Protects

How great is the goodness you have stored up for those who fear you. You lavish it on those who come to you for protection, blessing them before the watching world. You hide them in the shelter of your presence, safe from those who conspire against them. You shelter them in your presence, far from accusing tongues.
Psalm 31:19-20 NLT

As the rest of the world runs around in turmoil and fear, they will see God's blessings being poured out upon your life. He will always show His goodness to you, even amidst a crisis. He lavishes you with His protection. He wraps His protection all around you so that not one side of you is exposed. God commands His angels to guard you in all your ways, everywhere you go. They will lift you up so that you do not even strike your foot on a stone. What the enemy means to cause you harm, God will turn around for your good and his demise. God will shelter you and defend you when people come against you with false accusations. He will take care of His child. God will not allow anyone to harm you. He is your protection and your defense in every single area of your life. You can plant your feet on God.

DAY 351

You Will Soar

*He gives power to the faint, and to him who has no might
he increases strength.*
Isaiah 40:29 ESV

God knows there are days you feel like you cannot even get yourself out of bed. There are days when everything seems to fall apart, and you feel weak and vulnerable. He knows there are days when you just want to crawl away from the world and everyone in it and curl up in a ball and cry. God understands these days, and He does not condemn you for them. Jesus went through all the emotions you have gone through. God has given you emotions, and it is okay to feel those emotions. He just does not want you to get stuck in these emotions. The enemy would like for you to live there, but God has so much life for you to live. Feel these emotions, process through them with Him, and then let Him help you get up and strengthen you once again and move forward. You will be able to comfort others when they feel these emotions. God loves you so much, and He has compassion for you. God loves to take care of you tenderly and carefully. He will never be hard or harsh with you. He will never use brute strength or expect you to pull yourself up by your bootstraps. God will always be gentle and kind in His healing process. God is with you; hold on to Him, you will dream again, and you will soar high above these storms on wings like an eagle.

DAY 352

Filled To Overflowing

I pray that God, the source of hope, will fill you
completely with joy and peace because you trust in him.
Then you will overflow with confident hope through the
power of the Holy Spirit.
Romans 15:13 NLT

You can put your complete and total trust in God. He will never fail you or walk away from you. He will be your safe person. He will be the place you can run to and hide away when you need to. God will fill you with joy and laughter. He will cover you with His peace that passes all understanding. You can put all your hope in Him. God will not disappoint you. When you hope in Him, it is a firm foundation. It is an anchor for your soul. It gives you the strength to not give up, and to push through to one more day. God will fill you to overflowing with all you need to live this life with Him through His Holy Spirit who lives and breathes in you. You are complete and whole in this relationship with Him. Don't look to anyone else to complete you; you are complete. God loves you and cherish you.

DAY 353

Trace God's Handprint

Behold, it was for my peace that I had intense bitterness;
but You have loved back my life from the pit of
corruption and nothingness, for You have cast all my sins
behind Your back.
Isaiah 38:17 AMPC

There are times that you will go through things that, at the time, you do not understand. There are times you will question God's love for you. You will question if He is involved in your life personally or if He is a distant God. There will even be times that you will question if He is even real, and that is all okay. God can handle all those questions. However, once you get to the other side of the storm and things have calmed, you will look back and see that He was there all along, involved, and personal, loving and guiding each step. God was there holding back the enemy and setting boundaries he could not pass. You will be able to trace His handprint as He wove together a magnificent tapestry of beauty and love in your life. You will see that what you thought was for your bad was working towards your good. You will see that His love carried you and pulled you up out of the deepest, darkest pit and set your feet on solid ground and that you walked out stronger, better, purified in the fire, and learned intimacy with Him. You will see that He was not just working for today and this world, but for eternity.

DAY 354

Wherever You Go, God Is There

You go before me and follow me.
You place your hand of blessing on my head.
Psalm 139:5 NLT

You do not have to fear what is ahead of you, and you do not need to keep looking behind you. God has already gone ahead of you and prepared a way for everything. There is already a plan for every decision you will make. He has gone behind you and washed away all your sins. He has redeemed things and restored things so that your broken past cannot haunt you anymore.

God has surrounded you on all sides so that no matter what storm you are in, you are protected completely. When you turn to the right, He is there. When you turn to the left, He is there. When you go high in the mountains, He is there. When you go to the bottoms of the oceans, God is there. There is nowhere you will go that His goodness and love will not go with you. His hands of blessings are always upon you.

DAY 355

God Is All You Need

Whom have I in heaven but you?
And there is nothing on earth that I desire besides
you. My flesh and my heart may fail,
but God is the strength of my heart and
my portion forever.
Psalm 73:25-26 ESV

God is all that you need. When you are down to nothing and have no one left, you are still rich and not alone. You will never be alone or poor when God is with you. No one on this earth, absolutely no one, can love you as much as He does. God's love is unconditional. It is not based on your love for Him or your behavior. It is not based on what you can do for Him or what you can or cannot give Him. God loves you because He wants to, and He will always want to; even if you say you hate Him, He will still love you. You cannot outrun, His love. It will always chase you down. You can trust God with your heart and everything that concerns you. He will be gentle and kind to you. He will cover you in His presence and show you His glory. God will never let go of you. You are completely safe in His care. Trust Him with all you have; God will not fail you!

DAY 356

Enjoy The Ride

Live carefree before God; he is most careful with you.
1 Peter 5:7 MSG

Do not live your life bound by fear and worry. Do not live your life bound by rules that traditions and people put on you. Jesus died for you to be completely free. He died for you to be free from every power of the enemy, including the traditions of man. Jesus did a complete work at the cross. He stripped fear of its power over you. He broke every chain and pulled the harness off you. He broke the yoke from your neck, and now you can live completely carefree in this world. You do not have to hide in shame because shame has been broken. Let go of it all. Lay it all at the foot of the cross and leave it there for good. God loves you, and He is watching over you carefully. It is okay for you to enjoy your life. Dance in the rain. Sing that song at the top of your lungs. Laugh, love and play, even as an adult. Giggle like a child and enjoy every moment of this ride.

DAY 357

Always Was, Always Will Be

For your kingdom is an everlasting kingdom.
You rule throughout all generations.
The Lord always keeps his promises;
he is gracious in all he does.
Psalm 145:13 NLT

God is faithful. He is true. He will never fail you. He will do everything He said He would do. Nothing He has promised will be left undone. He will show you His kindness and favor in everything you do, everywhere you go, and everyone you meet. God will preserve you and defend you. He will do things in your life that will blow your mind and go way beyond your wildest dreams if you let Him. Trust God with everything! He is the Lord of lords and the King of kings! God is the Great I AM! He always was, and always will be. There is nothing God cannot do! He will have favor on whom He will have favor, and no one can reverse what He has planned. God is Holy and Righteous and Powerful, yet He is totally enthralled with you!

DAY 358

Mighty Oak Tree

He has sent me to tell those who mourn that the time of the Lord's favor has come, and with it, the day of God's anger against their enemies. To all who mourn in Israel, he will give a crown of beauty for ashes, a joyous blessing instead of mourning, festive praise instead of despair. In their righteousness, they will be like great oaks that the Lord has planted for his own glory.
Isaiah 61:2-3 NLT

God sent Jesus to set you free. Jesus was anointed to preach the good news, give beauty for ashes, and joy for mourning. He came to give praise instead of despair and make you righteous. He did all this so that you could, in turn, be anointed to preach the good news, to set the captives free, to give joy instead of mourning and praise instead of despair. God heals you and makes you whole, then He plants you, and you grow into a strong oak which brings Him glory and honor as you transform into the person, He made you to be. You shine for God. Your roots grow down deep into Him. You stand tall and strong and beautiful as His mighty oak tree.

DAY 359

Clear Path Ahead

Show me the right path, O Lord; point out the road for me to follow. Lead me by your truth and teach me, for you are the God who saves me. All day long I put my hope in you. Remember, O Lord, your compassion and unfailing love, which you have shown from long ages past.
Psalm 25:4-6 NLT

Seek God's face first in all you do. Ask Him, and He will help you to make wise and righteous decisions. God will show you clearly the path you should take. Instead of stumbling around trying to find your way on your own, ask God. He will lead you to the Truth. He will teach you His ways so that all may go well for you. God will save you and give you a legacy. Put your hope in God. Never let hope die. When hope dies, your vision dies, your faith dies. Don't let the enemy steal your hope. Always keep your mind on God's unfailing, unwavering, extravagant, marvelous love for you. His love cannot and will not fail you. Build your life on His love. It will drive out all your fears and be a solid foundation to build on. His love will not crumble under your feet. God will bless you when you live for Him, not only you but your children and their children, generation after generation.

DAY 360

God Will Keep You

*The Lord keeps you from all harm and watches over your
life. The Lord keeps watch over you as you come and
go, both now and forever.*
Psalm 121:7-8 NLT

God is your Strong Protector. He never takes His eyes off
you. He is constantly watching every side and all around
you to keep your life from harm. God goes before you, and
behind you. His sweet, protecting presence wraps around
you. God watches over you as you leave and as you come
home. He is with you both now and for eternity. Your
name is engraved on the palm of His hand. You are always
in His thoughts. God's thoughts toward you are good. Has
planned a promising future for you. A future with hope and
amazing things in store. Stay with God. Don't ever give up
on your dreams. He will watch over everything He has
promised you, and He will bring it to pass. Don't get in a
hurry; relax and enjoy this journey as you walk beside
God.

DAY 361

God Will Honor You

Nebuchadnezzar said, "Blessed be the God of Shadrach, Meshach, and Abednego! He sent his angel and rescued his servants who trusted in him! They ignored the king's orders and laid their bodies on the line rather than serve or worship any god but their own.
Daniel 3:28 MSG

When you stand firm for God, He will always reward you. God will hold back enemy armies for you. He will be your guard on all sides. When you choose God, even in the face of ridicule, persecution, or even death, you will have a great, great reward. God will cause His face to shine upon you. He will rescue you and honor you. He will cause everyone around you to know that His favor is upon you. They will see God do miracles in you and through you. He will never abandon those who put their complete trust in Him, even when the voices around them are trying to sway them not to. You will see mighty men fall, but those who trust in God will stand firm, for He will take care of them.

DAY 362

God Is Your Portion

See, God has come to save me.
I will trust in him and not be afraid.
The Lord God is my strength and my song;
he has given me victory."
Isaiah 12:2 NLT

When God is your God, you can walk boldly and with confidence. He is your salvation, your deliverance, healing, and forgiveness. He is everything you will need. God puts a new song in your heart. A song of praise and honor to Him. You can walk through this life unafraid, trusting every detail to Him. God knows what He is doing. He has a perfect plan for your life. Life may not always be easy, but no matter the circumstances, because He is your portion, you can walk in peace and be content during any storm. Whether you are rich or poor, in sickness or health, you will be sustained because He is yours, and you are His for eternity.

DAY 363

Jesus Sealed The Deal

Christ redeemed us from that self-defeating, cursed life by absorbing it completely into himself. Do you remember the Scripture that says, "Cursed is everyone who hangs on a tree"? That is what happened when Jesus was nailed to the cross: He became a curse, and at the same time, dissolved the curse. And now, because of that, the air is cleared, and we can see that Abraham's blessing is present and available for non-Jews, too. We are all able to receive God's life, his Spirit, in and with us by believing—just the way Abraham received it.
Galatians 3:13-14 MSG

Jesus took everything upon Himself for you. He was cursed so that you could be blessed. He absorbed all your punishment so that you could have a relationship with God. He was separated from God so that you could come close to Him and never be separated again. Now you are qualified for every single blessing from God. You receive everything now, not by your good works or your ability or strength, but simply by believing in Jesus. It is for freedom that Christ has set you free. Do not let the enemy put those chains back around you again. There is absolutely nothing you can do or must do to earn anything from God. He loves you unconditionally and unwaveringly. Jesus sealed the deal for you. It is finished!

DAY 364

God Is Not Far

"His purpose was for the nations to seek after God and perhaps feel their way toward him and find him—though he is not far from any one of us. For in him we live and move and exist. As some of your own poets have said, 'We are his offspring.'
Acts 17:27-28 NLT

God is right here with you. He is not far away or hiding from you. God wants you to draw near to Him. It is in God that you live and move and have your being. He is as close as your next breath. He will never leave you alone. You are His child, and He is captivated by you. God runs to you when He hears you call for help. Never feel like you must hide your face from Him. He will never condemn you or make you feel like you are not good enough for Him. God cherishes you, and you are precious to Him. The enemy will make you think God is mad at you when you sin or fail, but this is never true. God is always here for you. He is always kind and compassionate, and gentle with you. God adores you!

DAY 365

Extravagant Love

*Watch what God does, and then you do it, like children
who learn proper behavior from their parents. Mostly
what God does is love you. Keep company with him and
learn a life of love. Observe how Christ loved us. His love
was not cautious but extravagant. He didn't love in order
to get something from us but to give everything of himself
to us. Love like that.*
Ephesians 5:1-2 MSG

God gave everything for you! He did not hold back even
His most precious Son. God loves you with everlasting and
unfailing love. His love for you is so extravagant. He was
not cautious with His love. He did not tippy-toe around
with His love; God poured it all out for you when Jesus
died on a cross. He had to separate Himself from Jesus in
that moment for you. He didn't do all of this to get anything
from you, but because He wanted a relationship with you.
He wants you to learn to love others like this. Love with a
love that doesn't ask for anything in return but loves even
when they don't love you back. Give even when you don't
get anything back. Learn to live a life of extravagant love.
This happens as you and God walk this journey together
hand in hand, side by side, communing with each other all
along the way. You are extravagantly, marvelously,
wonderfully, forever loved!

Prayer of Salvation

It is my prayer that if you do not know Jesus, the One I have spoken about throughout this book, that you will open your heart to Him today.

God sent His Son just for you so that you could have a relationship with Him. Jesus died for you! He finished everything that is needed for you to approach God without fear. God is not mad at you, no matter what you have done or where you have been. You do not need to wait until you have it all together. Not one of us will ever have it all together. We are all just a bunch of imperfect people who need a loving and gracious Savior. Jesus is that Savior.

If you would like to know Him personally and enter this crazy, exciting, too good to be true relationship with Him, and have ALL your sins wiped away immediately, right now this very moment, just pray this prayer right where you find yourself today.

Jesus,

I believe you are the Son of God. I believe you came to earth, died on a cross, and rose from the grave. I put my faith in you today.

I ask you to forgive all my sins and make me a brand-new person inside.

I want to live this life with You and for You. I no longer want to try to do everything on my own. I declare today that You are the Lord of my life.

Thank You that I am now Your child, completely and totally clean and pure as I stand before You.

Help me live it out each day, keeping my eyes focused on Your finished work, knowing I could never do this on my own.

I relinquish control to You, and I rest in Your love for me. Thank You that I am extravagantly loved, accepted, and approved of right now at this moment, and I do not have to earn anything from You.

Amen.

Acknowledgements

Thank you, Jason, for always cheering me on even when I wanted to quit in the middle. You are my best friend forever! You always believe in me and know how to pull the potential out of me that God has placed within.

Thanks mom and dad for not letting me give up on my dreams and reminding me that God has called me, and He will work through me.

Thank you, Ms. Rosie, for praying for me and encouraging me that God has placed a gift within me and to never stop writing.

Thank you to my boys, my daughters-in-law, and all my family who encourage me, pray for me and love me unconditionally.

I would like to thank Ellen Sallas of The Author's Mentor, for once again making my book beautiful inside and out. Not only is she one of the best at what she does, but also a cherished friend. I am forever grateful to God for connecting us!

About the author

Gina Lynn Murray is an Amazon bestselling author and speaker. Gina's first book, *One Trembling Heart, Out of Darkness Into the Light: A Journey from Paralyzing Anxiety to Finding Rest,* received a 5-Star review from Reader's Favorite and hit Amazon's top 100 bestsellers list, as well as Amazon's top Hot New Releases.

Gina has also written two more devotionals entitled *30 Days of Resurrection* and *30 Days of Blessings for Moms.*

Gina has several other books that are in the process of being published and released. It is Gina's heart to pour God's love into broken vessels and see His children healed. She believes that even if one person is changed by her content, she has fulfilled God's purpose for her life.
You can find all of Gina's content on her website, ginalynnmurray.com. You can also find her on Instagram, Facebook, and YouTube.

Also by Author Gina Lynn Murray

Inspiration, Encouragement, Comfort

Devotionals for your Walk

findingrestmin.org
ginalynnmurray.com
Available at Amazon.com and other fine booksellers.